THE GOOD KARMA DIVORCE

THE GOOD KARMA DIVORCE

Avoid Litigation, Turn Negative Emotions into Positive Actions, and Get On with the Rest of Your Life

Judge Michele Lowrance

HarperOne
An Imprint of HarperCollinsPublishers

HarperOne

Throughout this book, I have used stories and examples designed to help the reader better understand the process. The stories are composites and the names have been changed to ensure confidentiality.

HarperCollins books may be purchased for educational, business, or sales promotional use. For information please write: Special Markets Department, HarperCollins Publishers, 10 East 53rd Street, New York, NY 10022.

HarperCollins Web site: http://www.harpercollins.com

HarperCollins®, ⬛®, and HarperOne™ are trademarks of HarperCollins Publishers

FIRST EDITION

Library of Congress Cataloging-in-Publication Data available upon request.

ISBN 978-0-06-184069-2

10 11 12 13 14   RRD(H)   10 9 8 7 6 5 4 3 2 1

To my son, Jonas

Contents

Note to Readers

Those who have lost love—the litigants in divorce court—and their lawyers have been my best teachers. But they will not recognize their cases or stories in this book, because I have scrambled genders, ages, and facts to ensure anonymity. I thank all the lawyers and litigants for those times when they allowed me to interact with them, offering me the opportunity to be held to a higher standard of wisdom and compassion. Many cases have haunted me, and the desire to shed light into the dark corners of participants' lives and the lives of other families is what inspired this book. I thank them for trusting me enough to reveal themselves and take a chance.

THE
GOOD
KARMA
DIVORCE

Introduction

How did I end up in this nightmare? I am a stranger to these dark emotions now living inside me. Who am I? When did I cross over the line, and will I ever cross back?

From across the bench I hear the whispers from their hearts. Beneath the fluorescent glare, the parties appear hostile, their arms tightly folded as if in straitjackets. A deputy stands behind them, menacingly, with a gun. These two people, who had once flirted, courted, and exchanged wedding vows, now seem to regard each other as kryptonite. I can see their hands trembling; my black robe often has that effect. Each comes to court with an agenda. Each seems determined to achieve vindication by convincing me of the other's loathsomeness. Then, and only then, can they ensure that the court punishes the guilty party for the personal wreckage they suffered. With the steam of hatred coming off their bodies like smoke from a greasy hamburger, they will attempt to raise children together.

I have been a judge in Domestic Relations Court in Chicago since 1995. For two decades prior to that I had sharpened my skills as a divorce attorney, but then I gave up being a warrior for the "right side," because it became clear to me that there was no right side in a divorce. Like "an eye for an eye," the only thing that happened in the end was that everyone was left with no eyes. As a survivor of divorce, my goal was to get through to this couple, and the thousands just like them, before they took the next step forward. How could I implore them to alter their perception of their divorce and of each other? Was there a way to restructure this heartbreaking life template that was being continually played out before me? If I could answer these questions, their lives might be affected positively. After years of experience, the answers to these questions have come into sharp focus, and the results are more profound than I could have ever expected.

What did I want for this couple? I wanted them—a husband and wife who had damaged each other, who had even devastated each other—to realize their anger would destroy them and infect every aspect of their future. I wanted them both to realize that this was what was happening. It finally struck me: they did not yet realize this. They had no idea of the extent to which their anger and resentment would injure those around them, as it damaged their own hearts, souls, and destinies. They had relinquished their strength by relying only on their attorneys and the court system to determine their future, oblivious to their own power over this potentially treacherous divorce process. There, in that forty-foot-square courtroom, this couple would either fuse with their anger, resentment, and bitterness or follow a path leading to peace through wisdom, understanding, and eventually forgiveness. They were facing a fork in the road that would change their lives forever.

The couples I see in my courtroom are desperately searching for emotional release; they smuggle their pain into their testimony, even when it is not relevant to the topic. They do so at every opportunity, hoping that somehow the court will know how to lessen their agony. In the end their desperate emotions remain unattended and unsatisfied. The sight of couples who participate exuberantly in a demolition derby always disturbs me. In an attempt to alleviate pain, even though the pain is transitory, they lash out, and irreparable damage is done. The court system was not built to house these emotions, and attorneys are not trained to reduce this kind of suffering. Divorcing people expect relief far beyond what the legal realm can provide from their attorneys and the courts, and they often end up feeling like members of a powerless, unprotected class. They are disappointed in their attorneys, and their attorneys are disappointed that they are not appreciated.

In my personal life, when divorced people discover I am a member of the judicial system, they are exploding to tell me how the system has failed them. People want to believe that life should be fair and bad things should not happen to good people. They expect emotional injustice to be righted by legal justice. The feeling that the rules of fairness have been violated leaves them limited choices on the emotional menu. Either they believe they did something wrong and blame themselves, or they think they were in the right and the administration of justice failed them. The unfortunate fallacy in believing that emotional injustice can be righted by the legal justice system creates anger and feelings of being cheated. This sense of being treated unfairly happens not just in those cases in which there was all-out warfare, but even in those in which disputes were eventually settled. Years after the divorce both groups of people understandably still have enduring bitterness and quiet, brooding grudges.

It began to dawn on me that divorcing people were often missing two things: a game plan and a Sherpa guide to direct them from the beginning to the end, while keeping them from falling into the crevasse on the treacherous journey. After all, how could anyone be expected to know the best way to unravel a marriage? In many ways my job is not just to decide futures or manage chaotic emotions, but to construct a master plan for broken families. What is the best approach to this process that is ultimately life-changing? How could it be shifted from a life-destroying ordeal to a more positive, transformational process? My professional and personal experience with divorce, combined with my studies in Eastern philosophy, led me to consider the law of karma and how to effectively apply it to the breakup and divorce process.

In Buddhism, good karma, or good action, comes back to you in countless ways. If you act graciously with compassion, you may receive compassion sooner or later, although you may or may not perceive it. But as you will see, your act of compassion changes who you are for the better immediately and is not dependent upon someone else's reciprocal behavior. The positive or negative outcomes of karma may not be immediate—they may take months, even years, to materialize—but if every action, good or bad, creates a reaction, why not allow good karma, or good action, to be your guiding principle?

If you are going through a divorce, I know you are terrified. If you are reading this book, I know you are already experiencing its destructive effects and are looking for answers. I want you to forget everything you think you know about divorce; your conventional wisdom will not serve you. I am going to suggest an approach that I have developed over fifteen years in my courtroom. The latest version, upon which this book is based, has had positive outcomes, case after case, for the last four years. You may think your divorce is unique. You may think that your problems are not solvable or that I can't possibly know your spouse. Here is what you need to know: nothing you can tell me will convince me that your divorce will not benefit from this approach, regardless of the circumstances.

You may not see another way through this ordeal. You may be too terrified to be open to something different. If you think there is no such thing as a Good Karma Divorce, then you have surrendered to the notion that you will be a victim at the hands of fate and you have no control when choosing your attitude about difficulty. That is tantamount to saying that there is no such thing as benefiting from difficult experiences, because destruction is inevitable.

As you contemplate how this book might work for you, you may be undergoing debilitating divorce stressors: the feelings of being misunderstood or unheard, the betrayal of friends and relatives, and depression so overpowering you can't even work. Perhaps there is a court order you can't pay or anxiety over the mounting legal bills, and you could be forgiven for thinking that your situation defies improvement. Most of the difficult cases that come into my courtroom start with the lawyers telling me, "Sorry, Judge, but this one will never settle." They then proceed to lay out their cases, which may center on money, children, betrayal, revenge, or any array of other seemingly unsolvable issues. Hopelessness, however, has no place in my courtroom. I simply don't allow it, and here's why.

In the most difficult scenarios, where the stakes are highest, the principles of the Good Karma Divorce are at their most profound. In fact, I respectfully reject the notion that there are any cases for which the Good Karma Divorce techniques are ineffective. I've been involved with numerous divorces in which one of the parties suffers from a mental disorder. Even then, with only one of the parties attempting the Good Karma Divorce principles, the collective suffering and conflict were substantially reduced. These principles, even if applied by only one of the parties, will exert a profound impact on the process, changing perspectives, attitudes, and ultimately the behavior of all involved.

I also want to state categorically that there is no expiration date on the Good Karma Divorce protocol. You might be in the middle of your divorce right now, or you might still be locked in mortal combat over a divorce that happened a decade ago. You can't completely eliminate the negative emotions or rewrite history, but you can discover a way to transform them into powerful thoughts and actions. At the very least, you do not want to compound your misfortune by sentencing yourself to further injury. Divorce does not need to be *the* defining moment for the rest of your life. I have seen this pain transformed, and considering the law of karma is a good start.

The process of choosing a Good Karma Divorce can lead you to a place of composure, wisdom, and bravery. I know that ideas like heroism, courage, and nobility are rarely associated with divorce or the breakdown of a relationship at any stage. However, I am proposing an alternative to the rigid view that divorce is the failure of an important life experience or that it is a life-destroying force that taints or ruins everything in its path. I know how agonizing the divorce process can be—it is like emotional surgery without anesthesia—but I have found that, because of the pain, people will go to any lengths to get out of it, even to the point of being open to a transformative opportunity. In court I have seen it in their eyes. People really want to have another way to feel or view their situation, but fear has locked them exclusively into survival mode. Survival mode will never deliver anything more than mere survival. You can help yourself, your children, and, if you desire, even your former partner with the principles of the Good Karma Divorce. It isn't just an anesthetic; it is a cure.

The Creation of a Negative Story Line

My early experiences have dominated my personal and career choices. Though I was not even three, I vividly remember hearing my parents speaking from the next room in a Miami hotel. They were getting a divorce and had just confessed to each other that neither had any interest in raising a child. "I don't want her," was followed by, "I don't want her either." I burst into their room and with angry tears said, "I don't want you either!" My mother and father were very young when I was born, and of course I didn't understand the stresses of being young parents—I just thought I wasn't worth sticking around for.

I don't need Freud to crawl out of his grave to explain why, when I sense trouble or abandonment in a relationship, whether real or perceived, I pull out the old familiar menu. The appetizer consists of creating emotional distance. By the entrée, I'm gone. My defenses, minted at an early age, are alive and well, and even though I understand this, I have overcome my history only with considerable effort and experience. Often a couple in my courtroom is fighting over who gets the children—unlike my parents, who were fighting over who wouldn't. In the end, the result is the same: neither couple is in the right mood to raise a child.

Divorce leaves its imprint in some way, but must it define and determine your future? Must you step into the old story line and be smothered by a gray quilt of annihilating perceptions?

There is inner pain: "I am a failure." "I wasn't able to keep my marriage together." "It's my fault; I should have tried harder." "I can't protect my children from the pain they are suffering, because I feel too depressed." "My marriage was how I defined myself in relation to the world—so who am I now?"

There is anger directed outward: "I can't believe how badly you're behaving." "You ruined our lives." "You aren't the person I married." "I should have known you'd do something like this." "How low of you to drag the kids into this."

Attachment to these story lines promotes a claustrophobic inability to imagine a positive exit from your union. This leaves little room for any ending other than one tinged with resentment, bitterness, and even hatred.

In some Asian philosophies, a destructive event or experience is often considered the prerequisite to the attainment of enlightenment. The crisis presents the opportunity to remove a blockage impeding your life's purpose. A Japanese proverb says, "My barn having burned to the ground, I can now see the moon." Believe it or not, sadness and even despair can have a positive effect, if those feelings ultimately loosen your attachment to a relationship that cannot bring you lasting peace and happiness. There's more than one story in every divorce, and there's room for more than one ending, if you make the effort with—or even without—your partner.

Too often, people think that being nasty, losing trust, acting angry, and feeling disappointed are as necessary to the process of divorce and separation as getting wet is to swimming. That view is reinforced by society throughout popular culture—in newspapers, on television, and in movies—everywhere divorce is depicted. But I believe we can create a culture in which divorce and separation, although absolutely not desirable, may be looked upon as an opportunity for transformation.

How to Rewrite the Story

Just because you're divorcing, your spouse isn't going to evaporate and cease to be. Particularly if you have children, this person will likely remain in your orbit and continue to walk the same earth you inhabit. You may think you are permanently leaving your spouse behind as you move forward into the next phase of your life, but the truth is that nothing—and no one—really gets left behind in an absolute way.

All of your shared experiences with your spouse—from tears of joy to tears of sorrow—make an indelible mark on your soul like a handprint in wet cement, whether you want them to or not. There are billions of people on earth, but you will come into contact with only a handful of them and have deep relationships with just a few of those. If you see yourself as a planet, whoever comes into your life is part of your solar system. A spouse with whom you share your life, for however long, is a major part of that solar system. Pain and suffering result when you tell yourself that the memory of your former spouse has no significance in your current life. The soul and the heart both know better, and in this tug of war peace may be elusive. Even long after you separate and divorce, this person and you will share a certain gravitational pull, and any children you have together will be permanent fixtures in your shared solar system. You can't fight that, and you may not be able to quiet the negative feelings that come up whenever you orbit too closely to your former spouse (even if you live thousands of miles apart).

Can you say unequivocally how your life is going to turn out? Isn't it possible it may turn out differently than the lamentable predictions made during this difficult time? Can you say your story line of the breakdown of your marriage is absolutely accurate? You can navigate crisis in a way that is life-enhancing, productive, and optimistic. To emerge from your breakup with this result, you will have to choose the road less traveled, to be different from those who experience divorce as complete destruction. You will find within yourself qualities and strength you didn't know you had. In accessing the power of understanding, gaining insights and patience, you will find yourself stretched well beyond who you knew yourself to be. These qualities might seem antithetical to the divorce process, and you might feel inclined to save these for a more worthy mate. But fortunately, you do not have to wait for your divorce to be over to uncover this new power and confidence. You can begin relieving your pain while enhancing your strength right now.

How to Use This Book and Access Good Karma

You might be anywhere in the separation or divorce process—from the very beginning to the "It's final" point. You might have a former partner you never or rarely speak to or one who communicates regularly and even cordially with you. (Communicating with your spouse or former spouse is not necessary.) You may be the initiator of this separation or divorce, or you may not even want it. You may or may not be a parent. You may be a grandparent, teacher, co-worker, friend, or neighbor of someone going through a divorce. Whether you were married for four months or forty years, whether you are friends with your spouse or never want to lay eyes on him or her again—even if you have been divorced for years and still haven't found peace with your situation, the principles apply. If your emotions are being triggered in any way by the divorce of anyone, this book is for you. You may want to have a transformation or an epiphany, make minor adjustments, or just be relieved from immediate pain. No matter where you are on this path, you can benefit from *The Good Karma Divorce*. Take what you need when you need to use it and leave the rest for later on, or put it on your bucket list.

Start with *Part One: Creating Your Soul Search Party*, in which you will learn how to prepare a Personal Manifesto. This Manifesto is the blueprint that will help carry you through the process. Your Manifesto, which you may also consider a flight plan, will keep you centered and on track as difficult and conflicting emotions and experiences arise that might draw you into a dark place. The Manifesto not only maintains your fuel reserves, but charts your destination. Only when you have a sense of your destination can you know when you are off course. There is an old fable about a frog placed in water that was slowly brought to a boil. Because he could not feel the temperature rising, he made no attempt to escape even as the water became hotter and hotter. Think of your Manifesto as a way of regulating your temperature, so that you don't wake up one day, cooked.

You will need a small journal or notebook (or use your computer, if you prefer) in which to create your Personal Manifesto as well as to answer the questions and do the exercises in Part One and throughout the book.

Part Two: Harnessing the Positive Power of Negative Emotions covers the range of negative feelings that most people going through divorce experience. No doubt you've heard of the seven stages of grief. Divorce brings its own set of stages, but we don't all seem to experience them in the same order. Because I believe that the act of criticism—whether we are on the giving or receiving end—is often the kickoff point for so many negative emotions, I begin with it. Criticism creates cracks in the strongest relationships.

Sometimes we learn to deal with criticism, and the cracks that form are only surface wear and tear; the relationship survives. Sometimes, however, criticism is the beginning of a much more damaging shift in the foundation of our marriage. The hairline cracks of criticism lead to other emotions, such as anger and resentment. Feelings such as depression, self-pity, loneliness, fear, and other aftershocks are covered in Chapter 6, "Mood Lighting: Emotions as a Source of Illumination." How can we turn these negative emotions into power and positive actions? Part Two strives to help you do just that.

Part Three: Preventing Collateral Damage is for divorcing partners with children, no matter what their ages may be. You can skip it if you are not a parent, but if you and your partner have children, they are as much a part of the divorce process as you are. People say things like, "Oh, kids are so resilient," which is code for, "They'll get over it." But an overreliance by anxious parents on this conventional wisdom contributes to a false sense of security that the children will be all right. Divorce is emotionally and psychologically devastating for all children, as decades of research bears out. Sometimes the impact of divorce on children is not seen until adulthood, but then it can manifest itself in many ways, from poor relationships to substance abuse and more. In this part I share my experiences in court and as a divorced mother and guide you on how to parent through these rough seas and protect your children, using the principles of the Good Karma Divorce.

Part Four: Transformative Confrontation deals with the nitty-gritty of courtroom confrontation (or face-to-face mediation) and how it can be handled with good karma. In it I draw on my experiences as lawyer and judge and share observations and survival strategies, including tips on what to say and how to say it (as well as when to stay silent).

Part Five: Embracing the Road Ahead helps you see past the divorce process and into the future. Chapter 15, "Karma and the Recycling of Human Relationships," offers hope, encouragement, and a philosophy for moving forward. The final chapter, "Building a Practice Circle," will enable you to widen your circle of support.

You can choose to remain angry, hurt, and resentful as you move through a breakup and divorce. Or you can do some digging and find within yourself qualities that may be forgotten, just waiting to be taken out and put to good use: your understanding, patience, compassion, and so many others. These traits may seem antithetical to those you would expect of a couple beginning the process of ending their marriage, but they are essential for turning your ending into your rebirth.

The Good Karma Divorce puts all your feelings and emotions to good use, no matter how negative or painful they may seem. Let its alchemy spin the ultimate marital crisis into golden healing for you, your former partner, and your children.

PART ONE

CREATING YOUR SOUL SEARCH PARTY

1

Your Personal Manifesto

The Antidote to the Negative Seductions of Breakup

Last night as I was sleeping,
I dreamt—marvelous error!—
that I had a beehive
here inside my heart.
And the golden bees
were making white combs
and sweet honey
from my own failures.
—ANTONIO MACHADO, *FROM "LAST NIGHT AS I WAS SLEEPING"*

You've just awakened and are sitting in the first chair you found, or if you're good to yourself you're sitting in your favorite chair, having your morning tea or coffee. The questions you are asking yourself deal with whether the destruction of your family or the loss of faith in your spouse is causing you to believe in nothing and no one: "Has the person I have always known been turned to dust, never to be found again? Yesterday I felt better, but today that anxiety is back—will I ever be out of pain? Does everyone around me see how badly I'm doing?"

Though you may have thoughts along these lines, can you make out that crack of light in the darkness that will allow for a more illuminating way to view your current circumstance? Is it possible that every new challenge, every new crisis is the modeling clay for building a new life, greater than you could ever have imagined? Can you envision that the loss of your marriage or relationship, no matter how bitter the pain, can be valuable to you in one way or another?

If you can start to ask questions like this—even if you can't yet answer them fully—you are on the road to turning your pain into a kind of power you may have never had the opportunity to access, the promise of something better yet to come. Poet Roger Housden puts it perfectly when he says, "The heart, like a grape, is prone to delivering its harvest at the same moment that it appears to be crushed."

The advent of a life crisis—breakup and divorce being among the most difficult—forces a person to choose a path. One direction can be destructive and therefore weakening, while another can build strength, wisdom, and awareness. At first it seems easier to behave any way you feel like—after all, you are hurt, you deserve it. Choosing a path with opportunities to build courage, compassion, and strength appears to require a fortitude you don't feel you can marshal. You might be thinking self-assessment is something you can do later, "after this is all over." The reality is the dark emotions of resentment, anger, hostility, and alienation from that person you know yourself to be contaminate the rest of your life, now and in the future. In this darkness it is difficult to see the life-enhancing lessons being offered.

You might say, "I want a peaceful divorce, but I don't feel it!" When it comes to divorce or separation and the ensuing implosion of the family unit, there are many easy-to-take paths that tend to be random, sloppy, and disordered. There are countless opportunities to create a cyclone out of a rain shower. There are no quick fixes—pain-free—when it comes to divorce. There are simply paths to take that are life-enhancing and others that are life-destroying. Sometimes circumstances provide a gentle nudge to find a higher path.

In the absence of "quick fixes," I started working on settlement techniques for reducing this pain and turmoil for the litigants in my courtroom. Interestingly, my investigation began as an attempt to flush out and then address all of the fears that blocked settlement in complicated child-custody cases. I asked the litigants to write down their worst fears concerning how their divorce would impact their relationship with their children, their concerns about the other party's parenting, and their ideal goals for their divorce. I began to notice that the sheer act of writing these down created a major shift in the litigants' emotional responsiveness and malleability in settling cases. I found that when fears were articulated, they could be addressed. Often a previously unrevealed fear lurking beneath the surface caused the emotional blockage that was obstructing the settlement.

The act of cataloguing fears and needs was so calming that people could move from an emotional to a problem-solving plane. In one instance, a case could not be settled because the wife was furious over her husband's affair with his office manager. Through writing, it became apparent that her real fear was that he would be obsessed with his new love and wouldn't see or support his children. She also feared being disposed of and disregarded, which activated her underlying fear of abandonment. We were able to write an agreement in which her husband agreed to almost every detail of communication that she required. He agreed to check in with her twice a week and not to bring his new girlfriend on custodial visits.

As I observed this phenomenon, I realized the secret was in having people *write down* their fears as well as their ideal goals or aspirations for themselves and their lives. Before my eyes, the couples were successfully mapping out what they previously had believed to be unchartable territory. I then researched the process of writing to find out why it made such a marked difference in the behavior of these couples. I was gratified to discover that neuroscientists had already solved this mystery. Through their research, it has now been demonstrated that writing employs different neurological pathways in the brain than those followed by cognitive thought. In short, by both thinking and writing about a fear we allow our brains to consider information from two distinctly different perspectives.

As cognitive neuropsychologist Dr. Leonard Miller tells us, "The process of writing activates the part of the brain that does the problem-solving and analyzing (the pre-frontal cortex), thereby deactivating the part of the brain where negative emotions like fear and anxiety are created."[1] One study conducted at the University of Texas found that writing about emotions improved physical health and immune function as well.[2] Other studies performed at UCLA showed that, just like hitting the brakes when you see a yellow light, you also hit the brakes on your emotional responses when you put feelings into words. Labeling fears and emotions decreases the activity in the part of the brain that creates fear and anxiety (the amygdala).[3] If you reduce fear, you can be more present, and if you can stay more present, you will stay in problem-solving mode. This enhanced ability to focus grants you immense power in the divorce process.

The couples in my courtroom were willing to write for two reasons. First, I made this exercise a requirement. Second, but more important, they intuitively knew they stood at a turning point in their lives. With uncertainty at its ripest, their fear of the uncharted territory of divorce made them willing to try something different. I don't like to let these rare opportunities go to waste. Through the Good Karma Divorce, you can have the power these couples found without having to appear in my courtroom. This resource is available to you and is dependent only upon your willingness to create a self-portrait using self-investigation coupled with the intention to reduce pain through more skillful methods. You will see that this writing does more than just reduce pain—it is a way to use your pain.

When you dump your emotions, concerns, and goals on the page, you free up much of the emotional energy you use to manage your feelings. Too often, this emotional content feels like something you chew and chew, but can never quite seem to swallow. With these circular thoughts on paper, you are free to focus on goal-setting and aspirational thinking. Writing will create what you will find is your most formidable ally in the divorce process—what I refer to as your Personal Manifesto. This document will be the tool you use to impose order on the disordered and chaotic experiences and emotions that lie ahead. You may think that goals and life purposes don't feel relevant to the pain you are in. But not to take command of your life plan is to allow the result to be guided by chance, which is no guide at all.

Physicists who study the nature of disorder believe it is largely predictable. They contend that the one thing you can always be certain of in the universe is an increase in disorder. Our technologically advanced society creates the illusion that we can control our lives. However, disorder is part of the natural order, and never do we feel more disordered than when our relationships and family seem to be falling apart. Here is your trifecta: the laws of natural disorder, the disorder of your own emotions, and the disorder of the emotions of everyone who matters to you. The mathematical odds of behaving in a way that promotes order and harmony may seem stacked against you.

Physicians, sociologists, theologians, psychologists, and philosophers all agree that divorce is one of life's greatest stressors, second only to the death of a mate or child. When it happens, you are presented with an array of opportunities, on an hourly basis, to decide what path in life you are going to take and which muscle you are going to exercise. Will it be the muscle of revenge and vendetta or is it the potent muscle of compassion and personal evolvement? Philosopher Friedrich Nietzsche said, "The most spiritual men, as the strongest, find their happiness where others would find their destruction: their joy is self-conquest."

Do you want to learn the lessons your divorce has to teach you? They are all there for the taking. Even if you believe that meeting your mate was a result of random occurrences, the relationship that resulted has great meaning because of the lessons it yields for you. Your lessons come through the choices you make, and your choices create your character. Elevating your wisdom, applying it, and sharing it with the people around you give meaning to your existence.

Creating a Personal Manifesto will solidify your intention to be the person you want to be, while shedding light on the path you're traveling and on the actions that got you to this point. It will become the architectural design of the positive path ahead of you and all the potential your future holds.

It is not easy to make this declaration, the essence of which is that every choice you make in life, every small step along the way, matters in your transformation. The high road is not the easiest path in the short run, but it is the least painful, and even when there is pain, you will be able to understand how it can benefit you. That understanding in and of itself reduces pain. Right now it might be easier to watch television than to do the transformational warm-ups that prepare you for a different mode of perception, but a temporary distraction like television will not help you access your power or give you sustained relief. It is often simpler to be reactionary, or just to follow the advice of your neighbor, than it is to take command of oneself. If you do not believe in taking this path just for yourself, then consider it a way to create a better life for your children and to minimize the psychological and emotional damage to them. Whether your mission is your personal enlightenment, protecting your soul from permanent wounds, or minimizing the damage to your children, you will be able to make sense of this tumultuous present and develop a view of the past that gives the future meaning.

A Personal Manifesto, or mission statement, is an organizing principle you will use to develop new perceptions and actions based on the core understanding that your old perceptions and actions may have created the problems you are now experiencing. Your Manifesto will become a sanctuary, a refuge, where you will be protected from the onslaughts of polluted thoughts about your divorce. On those days when you are feeling disconnected from your true self, distanced from your aspirational self (the person you would like to become), and almost completely stripped of optimism and hope, you will have in your drawer your self-made antidote pulling you away from the dark side. You will have created a psychological home that will always be available to you during times of vulnerability. Often the reading of one sentence can trigger a shift in your perspective and bring you back from the brink.

The process of developing your Manifesto creates your first shift in attitude. You will not only be sculpting your aspirational self; you will also be emphasizing positive emotions and qualities you can use to counter negative thought streams. Ultimately you will be able to assign meaning to the pain in your life, and you can start to envision the possibility that pain is not always destructive, but can be transformative. When you see pain in a new light, it changes your relationship to adversity. In time the Manifesto will become your personal doctrine containing your own investigated truth, so that when you refer to it, it will give you moments of inspiration and transcendence.

What Does a Personal Manifesto Look Like?

Let's start with this: the Personal Manifesto process is highly individualized. Yours won't necessarily look like anyone else's. There are no rules, just guidelines to get you started and something I call "transformational warm-ups"—a series of questions to get you thinking and to shake up your perspective.

Remember, it's all about figuring out where you are now, then deciding where you want to go and who you want to be when you get there. So shed your inhibitions, discard conventional wisdom, banish fear, and *get started*.

(If you're someone who needs to read other chapters first, that's fine too. Just remember to come back to this chapter when you're ready. I cannot overemphasize the importance of the physical act of getting the words on paper. The velocity of your journey toward healing and growth depends upon it. I have tested this process hundreds of times, in and out of my courtroom, and it works.)

Your Personal Manifesto can be half a page long or a dozen, although I think once you get started you'll probably find you have a lot to say. You may find yourself writing things you've never articulated to anyone—not even your former spouse or your closest friend. Keep this work in a safe place so you can be brutally honest and completely unself-conscious.

As you begin, expect to create a series of lists, punctuated by the occasional revelatory moments. Don't stop writing until you get it all out. Grammar doesn't matter. Neither does spelling or penmanship. No one should ever see these early drafts but you. That being said, this is probably an appropriate place for us to talk about what is discoverable in a divorce action. Many people do not realize that unless it is part of a document you send to or work on with your lawyer, anything you write could be subpoenaed if relevant. This includes your diary, a letter to your sister, even your emails.

Obviously, early rambling drafts of your Manifesto in which you rant, rage, and vent are included. I would destroy the early drafts once you've finished with them, particularly if they contain thoughts, self-evaluation, or destructive fantasies you would not want spoken aloud in a courtroom. (However, if a litigant produced documents in my courtroom that showed that his or her former spouse was trying to be a better person and to learn from the divorce, imagine how favorably the creator of those documents would appear—and how mean-spirited the one who had dragged the documents into court.)

You may fear taking on another project—to develop your Personal Manifesto—because you don't think you have the energy reserves for it. But remember, most of your energy is tied up in your current state of emotional upheaval. Once you transfer your thoughts onto paper something interesting is going to occur neurologically. Your brain, relieved of some of its policing duties, won't have to fight so hard to impose order on chaos and now it can shift into clarity and creative problem solving.

Before we move on to the transformational warm-ups, I have a few other comments about the process you are about to begin.

1. Your Personal Manifesto will be revised several times before you get to the working document. Do not worry about perfection—striving for perfection can be the insidious enemy of getting this done, particularly because the work to be done is emotional in nature.

2. As you continue with the chapters in this book, further revisions may become necessary or desirable, so don't focus on getting to that unattainable "final" product.

3. Some readers may feel what I am describing is nothing more than keeping a journal or diary. Wrong. Journaling over a period of time may be a healthy and revealing habit. However, it differs significantly from the process of creating your Personal Manifesto because although your first draft feels like journaling, that is merely the starting point. The first draft provides the baseline for growth. The next drafts start to layer analysis and revelation on top of experience and emotion, and frankly, that's where the real power becomes accessible. The reward for this work is not only power, but also strength. Chaos and confusion is the soil from which your Manifesto will be born.

4. The goal of your Personal Manifesto is healing and growth, and for that, you need to document where you've been, where you are now, and your aspirations for where (and for whom) you will be tomorrow. This process works, whether we fully understand it or not. The nexus for change appears to be located precisely at the point the words move from thoughts to your hand to the paper or computer screen.

Transformational Warm-ups: Getting Started on Your Personal Manifesto

I am now going to suggest a series of questions designed to get you thinking honestly about your current mental state. Have you ever noticed that we often eulogize someone after death, even if that person meant little to us in life? We do that as individuals, and as a society, even if the person in question led a life not exactly deserving of sainthood. It's as if the mysterious process of death somehow confers a right to the benefit of the doubt.

However, when the loss is as a result of divorce, we often behave very differently. No matter the rich and velveted moments we may have shared, most of us give in to an irresistible temptation to focus only on the negatives. You'll often hear me talk about the dangers of writing off an entire relationship just because it ends in divorce. While a former mate may well be replaceable, the moments shared are not. The totality of moments shared with that person carry parts of us that cannot be replaced—ever. Whether we like it or not, that former mate is in our bloodstream, and always will be. In his or her face, we see a mirror of our past. We actually sabotage our own healing when we reduce former partners to mere sound bites, as in "My ex-wife is a total bitch," or "My first husband was a chronic liar."

As you begin the Personal Manifesto process, allow your writing to recognize both the good and the bad in your experiences with your former mate. Understand that we don't have to corrupt good memories in order to detach. Allow yourself to take into account your own multidimensionality as well as that of your spouse. Good thinking can become clogged with sabotaging thoughts and fears. Fears usually fade, but without a way to harness them, they can wreak havoc before they make their exit. Your Manifesto helps you to get a more balanced picture of the data before your story takes on such a negative form that you find it difficult to move beyond it. As you begin your investigation, you want to make sure you have not been tampering with the evidence.

With that observation in mind, let's start the process of self-discovery. As you think through the following transformational warm-up questions, write out your answers and make notes on how you feel as you are writing, including any insights that emerge.

1. Recall five things about your mate that you once treasured. Write these things down in as much emotional detail as possible, as you will use this information to balance yourself emotionally during periods of conflict and adversity.

2. Write down at least five offenses your mate has inflicted upon you. Did you retaliate? Did you play any role in or have any responsibility for those encounters, no matter how small?

3. List at least five offenses inflicted upon you by your mate that you have not mirrored to either your spouse or others. (Bet you can't!)

4. Picture and describe the kind of person you want to be now. How do you want to remember yourself five years from now, when you look back at what you were like during your divorce or breakup? Do you want to remember yourself as a whiner, swimming in self-pity, vengeful, and petty? Or as someone who attempted to withstand this difficult transition along with its challenges with dignity?

5. If you can stand it, have someone take a picture of you when you are feeling really angry. Then take a good look at yourself in that photo. You are certainly entitled to look and feel that way, but ask yourself how many times you want to relive that moment, how long you want that image to last. In what ways do you aspire to shift from how you appear in that image, and are you willing to do some work to make that shift?

6. Make a list of five heroes, real or fictitious, and next to each name write three things you like about each one. What things do you have in common with them?

7. If you are a parent, list all the positive qualities you think a good parent should have. Next to each put a plus sign if you think you have that quality and a minus sign if you think you don't. Look at the qualities with minuses, and next to them write down why you think you do not posses these qualities. Are they essential qualities that apply to you and your children? If so, are these issues you can work on? Write down how you would like your children to describe you now. How would you like them to describe you five years from now? When they are independent adults?

8. Describe the ideal way you would like to handle your disappointment and resentment.

9. What are the three greatest benefits you've reaped from your relationship? How has your relationship shaped you and contributed positively to the person you are today?

10. Make a list of things you are waiting for, things you want to have happen in your life before you can believe it is "good." Next to each item, note whether your former spouse is keeping you from that goal or otherwise stopping that event from coming to pass. (Look at your list now and note how much power you may be giving to your former spouse.) Next to each item, write down a word or phrase describing how it feels to be waiting.

11. Write out your doubts that you can find peace and resolution by taking the path of the Good Karma Divorce. Write down why you think you have difficulty accepting the idea that you can minimize your suffering. For example: "I don't believe I can find peace as long as my husband screams at me and has cut me off financially. I don't believe I can find resolution while I'm juggling all these worries."

12. How could you change such statements? Try reframing your negative thought patterns by shifting some attitudes. For example:

"Though I believe it may be difficult to find peace, I don't have to engage in anger and reciprocate negative emotions when my husband screams at me. I can teach myself not to react or to disengage by hanging up the phone. Though I won't learn to do these things overnight, I can still start to change my behavior. I will look for other avenues of financial support, including through the courts. I will have faith that this situation is not frozen and that I will move beyond this phase of my life."

The above warm-ups are useful for a number of reasons:

1. You are able to discover how you are thinking before you begin to problem-solve. You can look at your automatic and reflexive state of mind.

2. You have identified your negative state of mind while reactivating positive memories, which are at the moment eclipsed by the negative. Recognizing the dominance of negative attitudes helps your brain get into the mood to make positive changes.

3. The questions inspire you to uncover how this mental state may have *not* served you, and in doing so you might decide to change it. If it has not served you, you might be willing to silence that negative thought stream to make way for something else.

4. If you can see where it has not served you, you might yield to a less destructive interpretation of your current situation. Science tells us that using multidimensional perspectives keeps our brains agile, so negative thoughts do not become embedded in them. That agility, developed while making these lists using novel or alternative thought processes, will help you get through the divorce process—and the rest of your life.

5. In creating this alternative interpretation, you have become an actor instead of a reactor; you have interrupted your own negative patterns, removed much of the clutter, and thereby advanced your control of your own mind. You now can create a real intention.

Writing Your Personal Manifesto

The transformational warm-ups you've just completed should have helped you to put in words your current emotional state. Now comes the interesting part, as you take each fear or negative and reframe it in a way that puts you back in control.

For example, a warm-up statement for you may be "I worry all the time." To convert that into an aspirational statement for your Manifesto, you might write "I don't want to be paralyzed by worry." If you feel that anger is a dominant factor in your emotional state, your Manifesto might say "I don't want to be controlled by my anger."

Your Personal Manifesto may include any or all of the following:

* How you feel in the present
* Habitual and reactive behaviors you want to change
* How those changes will benefit your life
* The kind of person you would like to be
* Acknowledgment of your progress
* A statement about self-forgiveness for your setbacks
* Your intentions for your future
* A statement motivating yourself to keep going on this path

Trying to live up to the aspirational portions of these sentiments should be the heart of your mission. Some days you will do better than others, but on those days that are challenging—between the life that was and the life that will be—remember that you have created a team of thoughts to protect you against your own negative impulses. Use your Manifesto as your mantra to get back on your chosen path and perhaps find an even better path.

Don't be surprised if the development of your Manifesto occurs in several stages. You won't have perfectly polished statements, of course, but you will have the beginnings of an important message to yourself.

The first attempt at writing your manifesto is more like a dumping of the poisons on the page. Until you do that, it's hard to think straight. Here's a first draft:

Sample Personal Manifesto: First Draft

September 15

I am in a slow, deep, seething boil. I can think of nothing else but how unfair my husband, John, has been. I am consumed with anger and resentment. One minute I'm so angry I want to kill him, and the next I'm paralyzed with fear and sadness. I want to make him suffer—I want him to pay. I want to call his boss to tell him what an unethical person John is. I know things that could probably get him fired. And her. She doesn't know what a manipulator he can be. I know how charming he is in the beginning. I'm throwing his stuff out in the driveway—including his Viagra pills. I can't stop thinking about the day Dan was born. We loved each other so much. He was so sweet to me and so proud of his boy—I did everything to make him happy. What did I do wrong? Maybe I didn't try hard enough—maybe I was too critical. I can't sleep at night, and I can't get out of bed in the morning. I am writing this with a faint hope that I can find a different way to handle this.

Sample Personal Manifesto: Second Draft

December 19

In the first draft of my Personal Manifesto I sound like a tortured animal. I do not want to be that person! It still hurts, and I'm still angry, but I have to be careful and not end up like Veronica, who can't stop spewing about her divorce. I want to come out of this divorce with dignity and self-respect. I won't stoop to his level. I don't need to get even or hurt him, although I admit I still have fantasies about it. This morning on the news there was a car crash in Elmwood Park where he works. My heart stopped,

*as I feared he was hurt. When I found out it wasn't him, I was
disappointed. Apparently some days I am doing better than
others, which is fine. I need to move forward in the most positive
way I can.*

*For the sake of the children, I am going to have to find a way
to interact with him—to be at least civil when we have to see
each other. I read the chapter on forgiveness and I am not sure
I can ever forgive him or his trailer-trash girlfriend. I need to
read that chapter again. I didn't cause him to be unfaithful,
and I'm going to try not to agonize over it when I should be
focusing on the future. I am so worried about money, and I will
do what I must to protect the family, but I don't want to take the
low road.*

*I know I am going to have good days and bad days, but these are
the things I want to be:*

- *a person of dignity and grace*

- *a mother who does not want her children to feel sorry for her*

- *a person who does not want her children to suffer just because she
  is angry*

- *a person who can forgive without feeling weak*

- *a person without regrets who can forgive herself for mistakes or feeling fragile and tired*

- *a person who does not fear self-knowledge, knowing that it is the
  way out of pain and on to a better future*

Note the change to a more reflective tone in the second attempt.
The writer is calmer, and her thoughts are directed more toward where
she is going. She is starting to develop mile markers of her progress.
She is also starting to notice her own patterns. The defining quality of
this draft is the shift from emotional venting to clearer, more focused
aspirational thought. Notice how she gains confidence and clarity in
the next version of her Manifesto:

Sample Personal Manifesto: Third Draft

July 17

I know I need to see our divorce for what it is—not as a failure, but as a personal evolution. Maybe he was to blame, but I am not going to make myself crazy by focusing on that. But we have a shared history, and for the sake of the children, I can't just throw that away. I am learning to value what was good.

I want to be able always to look back and be proud of how I handled my divorce. I want to be the hero in my own life, someone who doesn't act on the negative feelings. But when I do, and I will, I will take responsibility for my thoughts and actions—even if I admit that responsibility only to myself. I visualize myself as a soldier, complete with valor and dignity.

No matter how depressed I might feel, I will drag myself to my dance class and be okay with having a terrible class. I can just be proud that I went. Every time I do what I didn't think I could do, I become stronger.

When I have a negative thought about John I will fuse it with a fond memory. I know many days I will have to dig to access one, especially after court. I may think it is easier to get over the divorce by focusing on the negative, to help me justify it, but then I am not being honest with myself. My marriage was as much good as it was difficult. I knew what our problems could be, and I didn't want to admit it to myself. The illusion of perfection was strictly of my making.

I will act with respect toward him, but that does not mean I have to concede what I believe is right for me. I understand that John has needs, but that does not mean I have to give up my own. I do not have to sacrifice what I am entitled to in order to show compassion for my former partner's struggle. For the first time I can see that his life is far from perfect. When I ask him for what I need and he says no, I will not take it personally, as I understand that he has needs as well. (This will really be tough for me, as I tend to think my needs are far more pressing!)

When my friends ask me what happened, I will resist painting myself as the victim. I also will resist implying to my children that I am the victim, even though it's pretty tempting to do so, as I could get extra attention that way. I want to set a heroic example for my children about how to behave during adversity. I know they are watching my every move.

Every choice I make takes me one step closer to or farther away from who I want to become. Even if I behave in ways I am not proud of in the morning, that doesn't mean I have to continue them throughout the day. I will forgive myself for those actions and just try to do better.

Fortifying Yourself and Your Manifesto

It can be challenging to create and preserve a Personal Manifesto in the face of a culture that supports aggression and anger as valuable components of a divorce strategy. There are times when you will need to be strong enough to fight against criticism from people around you who believe you should see your divorce as a holy war. You may have to protect yourself from being derailed by your friends who have just chipped in to buy you the commemorative DVD of *The War of the Roses*. Julia Cameron, author of *The Artist's Way*, calls it "drawing the sacred circle around new behavior; because it is new, it is quite fragile."[4] I suggest that if certain people do not support your new behavior, just don't talk about it with them. This path, together with its fortification, which will be discussed in later chapters, is a way for you to maintain personal power regardless of the chaos that appears to surround you.

I know it's difficult to think about creating something like the Personal Manifesto when you don't know where you are going to live, how you are going to pay your bills, whether you will have a mate again, or how to lift your children out of depression. But your Manifesto is vital, because it creates the window through which you can see the rest of your life, and it is the antidote to the negative seductions of the divorce process.

Very often I hear people say things like, "If only this case would settle—then I would find happiness." What this really means is, "My happiness is dependent on my spouse's agreement." But why wait? Why not take a path *now* that will lead to your happiness? Being content and finding peace—even in the midst of the divorce process—should not hinge solely on the behavior of another individual. You don't have to sentence yourself to wait. You can start sculpting that strong, powerful person you can be right now. The average divorce takes two years—imagine what you could accomplish during that time.

The aspiration toward a good karma divorce in the face of adversity is the underlying theme of your Personal Manifesto. Perhaps you gagged or rolled your eyes at one of the transformational warm-up questions, the suggestion that you write down the names of your heroes—those men and women, real or not, who display the kind of character you admire. This was meant to get your aspirational juices flowing, but there's a deeper purpose at work here too.

People gravitate toward heroes who display traits like bravery, compassion, and dignity, particularly those who show grace under pressure. You are inspired by their fortitude. When you choose to be heroic, you are inspired—and in turn you can inspire. As I said earlier, experiencing a divorce doesn't necessarily conjure up images of heroism, but desiring the character of a true hero is precisely what will get you through your darkest days.

Ralph Waldo Emerson said, "Sow a thought, and you reap an action; sow an action, and you reap a habit; sow a habit, and you reap a character; sow a character, and you reap a destiny." The character created through adhering to your Manifesto and attempting some of the principles of the Good Karma Divorce are the building blocks of your destiny—and not only your destiny, but the destinies of your family, your former partner, your friends and loved ones, virtually everyone you come into contact with, and everyone who comes into contact with them. This newly forged person you will become will enhance the legacy of your emotional DNA for your family during this generation and for generations to come.

When following your Manifesto, fortified by reading the chapters that follow, you will experience micro shifts in behavior. The transformation will start subtlely. Instead of calling your former spouse a liar, you refer to him or her as not always accurate. When you hear yourself exaggerating a story about your former spouse's "bad" behavior as you vent to a friend, you check yourself. When you have done something for which you must apologize, you don't wait for the other person's resentments to harden. You pick up the phone, take a deep breath, and dial— you now sense that it's so much better for everyone involved if you do it sooner rather than later. It only takes small shifts, merely little poppy seeds of change. On many days your Manifesto will outshine you. It is of great value even if you do not fully attain your goals. It is enough if it fosters inspiration. As in a sport that requires aim, the thing that matters is keeping your eye on the target.

Finally, remember that adhering to your Manifesto can reduce your fear of "being found out," even if you've done absolutely nothing wrong. When you're going through a divorce, complete with attorneys, legal papers, and proceedings, in the face of all this authority and officialdom you can still feel as though you're "in trouble." Under that microscope you may have a lingering feeling that something you've done, ten years ago or ten days ago, will be revealed in a deposition or in a trial. But your Manifesto can protect you.

In one of my cases a couple was in a troubling custody battle. The father alleged that the mother had been neglectful of the children and was going out five nights a week, sleeping late in the morning, not getting the children to school on time, not keeping up with the children's medical exams, and not going to PTA meetings. The psychiatric evaluation confirmed the allegations, but noted concerns about recommending that the father have custody, because the children were more bonded to the mother and would be devastated if custody were transferred. The father really didn't want to take the children from their mother, but felt he didn't have a choice. The mother was terrified and was willing to do anything to keep residential custody. To find a productive middle ground, we worked out an entire protocol for better parenting. This included therapy for the mother and her informing the court about her progress and her difficulties through the children's attorney. This became a Manifesto by court order long before I had a name for it. The parties eventually worked out a joint parenting order based upon the father's being satisfied that the mother was really devoted to changing.

With caution, and by reviewing it with your attorney, you may even bring your enhanced version of your Manifesto into the light (yes, if you are being viewed in a negative light, you can testify about its current importance). Its very existence is proof that you are setting out on a higher road. It's proof that your goal is not to cause pain and seek revenge, but to protect your family—perhaps including your former spouse—from the destructive, life-damaging forces of divorce. It's proof that you have the character of a hero.

2

The Process

Reclaiming Your Power

There was a man who was very troubled: he was having
problems with his children, his finances were in
terrible shape, his crop had failed, and his wife was
in very poor health. He traveled far and for many
months to see the Buddha to talk about these problems.
When he finally arrived, he met with the Buddha,
and after he explained his dilemma, the Buddha
said, "I cannot help you." The man asked, "How can
that be true? After all, you are the Buddha!" To this
the Buddha responded, "At any point in your life,
or in anyone's life, there will always be 71 problems.
The only thing that I can help you with is the 72nd
problem, and that is how to deal with the 71 problems."
—Ancient Buddhist parable

My second husband and I decided to separate in the April rain
on a Friday afternoon. By Saturday morning, like Scarlett
O'Hara when she made her famous proclamation never to be
hungry again, I made a vow. No matter what turn my case would take
(I now was also a case), I would handle myself differently from the many
couples I had seen both in and outside of my courtroom. I had seen the
ravages of the divorce process carved into their war-torn faces. Over
time their skin had grayed, and even their hair hung sadly. I have seen
people behave in ways they would later tell me they were ashamed of.

I knew what was coming for me; the temptation to be petty and vengeful would be immense. I wanted this life crisis to be defining for me. I wanted to be proud of how I acted, and I didn't want to whine, weep, and wilt. I wanted to show grace under pressure. It was my job to be the cartographer, to map the person I was going to be when this was over. Poet and critic James Russell Lowell said, "There is no good arguing with the inevitable. The only argument available with an east wind is to put on your overcoat." I wanted to figure out what kind of protective gear I would need to construct. Like it or not, I put on that overcoat every day. Sometimes I would feel warm and sheltered, and at other times the overcoat felt like a straitjacket.

Every monumental journey requires enormous courage and inner strength to deal with the onslaught of fear, doubt, and uncertainty. Because divorce is experienced as an avalanche upon the soul and the emotions, people move directly into survival mode. In survival mode we try to bury the pain, and in so doing we also bury good memories along with the bones of the marriage. Now any remnants of affection must be buried alive, still twitching. This is the time when there is often devotion to any propaganda that devalues our spouse. Although survival mode has short-term utility, it can be destructive if sustained for extended periods of time.

The breakup did not happen overnight. A thief did not steal your love in the dark. Brick by brick, the house of love was dismantled. One brick was trust, a second was loyalty, another was sharing core values, and so forth. Compounded and repetitious negativity has become so dominant that we fear we are losing the person that we know ourselves to be. Most of us know ourselves to be kind, but now we are having trouble accessing and maintaining our true self. When the mind is crowded by negative fears and thoughts, it soon takes on the character of that negativity. As a society, we have embraced all things green. We now abhor waste—we recycle everything from cell phones to the cardboard core inside a roll of paper towels—and we think twice before we throw something away. Are broken marital relationships the one area of life exempted from the concept of recycling? Are we so obsessed with hiding evidence of this so-called failure that we have no choice but to throw out the good with the bad? Through negativity, are we ready to exclude a former spouse from any further purpose?

Recycling is a philosophy—that in everything there is further purpose and possibility. Is it possible that this also applies to a former spouse? As we shall see, he or she may well turn out to be our greatest teacher.

In order to maximize your life experience and minimize self-destruction and harm to those around you, you need a game plan with organizing principles. Society has traditionally viewed divorce as a process that insists on antagonism and opposing forces. Consequently there are hardly any reassuring guideposts to help you see that there is a way to success other than "winning a battle." Whether or not you understand how the process described in this book works, the chapters, as guideposts, will show you a new way to perceive your reality. But for those of you who like to know where the side rails are when you scale the cliffs, here is how the process I am suggesting usually goes, in the order of occurrence:

- The journey to enlightenment, according to Buddha, "does not begin with the teaching on the beauty of enlightenment." It is important to explore first why you are suffering—and to understand that it is not simply because you are going through a divorce.
- After this exploration, you will seek the skills you need to maintain your former self—and to resist attaching to negativity. You will even come to see the value of your spouse in your life experience, and you will find that there are ways to detach that are far more effective than the evisceration of good memories. You used to hold your relationship in the hands of love. When love appears to have left the relationship, why not hold it instead in the hands of good memory?
- You want to reduce the destruction to yourself and those around you by unhinging the power of negative emotions. You will come to understand that each emotion offers ripe opportunities for shifting your perception about your circumstances and your spouse.
- As you experience crisis in an innovative way, you will see the possibilities of building an enhanced state of being. You may

never have asked yourself questions about who you want to be and whether you are in alignment with those desires. You may start to wonder if building on this perceptual shift could open limitless possibilities in your life. How far up the ladder can you climb now that you have ascended that first rung successfully? As you taste the limitless possibilities, having found new mental dexterity, you will now dare to ask yourself what new meaning your life might have.

- When you have reduced the noisy clamor produced when you are trying to hold on to how you think things should be but aren't, you can hear the whisper of who you really are. You may find the person you have always known was there inside, but have not taken the time to attend to and develop. You may begin to find an alignment between who you are, who you want to be, and your true life purpose.

Ultimately, people crave authenticity. Most truly want to live according to their core values. In divorce, however, these same people often lose their way without even realizing how far off course they have drifted. "When did you lose yourself?" is a question I frequently ask in court. "When did you stop being the person you thought you were?" The heartrending and bewildered response is almost always a variation on "I don't know," and even the manliest of men fight back tears in the face of this scalding realization. Hemorrhaging sadness, they can't quite remember where they've left themselves, and they fear they can never find their way home again.

I ask them: "When did you both give up what you believed in? When did you become people who are now defined by their reactions to the conduct of another? I know that neither of you is the person that I am seeing today. When did you lose your desire to be optimistic and vital? When were you no longer able to summon up your better selves? You have given each other more power than they could have ever taken." When the husband and the wife both had tears in their eyes, I saw true soul devastation. They had given up their core values in the process of divorcing. I of course was satisfied, because they went from mad to sad. That sadness was real; the "mad" in this case was a diversionary emotion. Now they were in a softer frame of mind, where the case could be settled.

A Process Rather Than a Flash of Inspiration

Buddha found that his answers and wisdom came to him not when he was fighting for answers (survival mode), but at those times when he stopped struggling to find them. Can you cease the struggle for momentary relief to consider the possibility that there may be another way of thinking? The art is in not acting upon emotions on first impulse. Your negative emotions need processing, like unpasteurized milk, so the bacteria and contaminants can be neutralized. Achieving this control over your emotions is much like practicing a golf swing. Practicing will not ensure that you will hit a hole in one; you can only ensure that you will practice three days a week. This is a time when behavior needs practice. How people respond to you may not be within your control, nor does it matter. With practice you will feel better regardless of the feedback you get from your mate. Practicing creates space between your reflexive behaviors and behaviors based on a new way of thinking that holds infinitely more possibilities for your future.

People may say, "Let it go," as if you could automatically go from a reflexive response to letting it go without processing. People tell you to "get over it," because they believe you should be on their timetable. But the more you do the exercises and follow the suggestions in this book, moving away from rigid and toward more fluid thought patterns, the more you actually reduce your struggle and the faster you "get over it."

You may inherit money. You may win the lottery. You may find love at first sight. But when it comes to wisdom, there are no shortcuts. There is no easy advice, and by the time you are done with your divorce, you will not be the same. But depending upon how you go through your stages, you can affect your desired outcome. You don't need a book to tell you that you are having a difficult time, but you may need help figuring out how to make penicillin from the mold. Suffering, unfortunately, is integral to finding out your life's purpose. Without suffering you may never do the work required to align yourself with that purpose. When you can give meaning to your suffering and acknowledge its transformative powers, you have changed your relationship to the life process. By now you know that life always contains suffering, and you will rarely have a dull moment. You can use the ways of reacting you're going to learn here as protocol for all difficult experiences.

Each chapter of this book is about another aspect of the stages we must go through, and each stage features its own snares and unique benefits. As you journey through the chapters, you will find out why each of these stages is crucial to the healing process. The exercises in the chapters allow you to become familiar with your starting point where ego-driven behavior has yet to be censored or disguised. It is easier to get a firm grip on where you are going when you know where you began. Only by looking at your spontaneous answers in the exercises can you glimpse your incremental progress. If you start with difficult concepts too soon (like the unthinkable forgiveness), they may seem unattainable. Or you may come to expect miracles. When the miracles don't happen, you risk sabotaging or abandoning the process and may seek immediate legal advice from Jack the Ripper. No matter how unpolished or negative your immediate responses may be, do not condemn them. They are just for observing what is revealed.

The problem with the high road is that the altitude can wear you out, especially when you're wearing that fifteen-pound halo. Changing emotional habits is as exhausting as learning how to drive a car on the left side of the road. Therefore, the process must be taken in in small pieces, so that each bite can be digested before the next one. It is hard to imagine taking a leap of faith that goes from a prison of pain to a free life. You can't think your way into that large a step. Without this pain you would never be inclined to do the work that it takes to get to your life's true purpose. Look at it this way: you are going through a divorce, and you are already in pain, so you might as well use it. As philosopher and poet Henri-Frédéric Amiel put it: "You desire to know the art of living, my friend? It is contained in one phrase: make use of suffering."

The exercises and suggestions in each of the chapters respect the fact that change must occur slowly. I suggest you marinate in one chapter for a while before going to the next. The exercises tend to flush to the surface negative patterns more rapidly than mere contemplation, accelerating your learning curve, so you may need time to absorb the lessons before you put them into practice.

I am not suggesting that you try to extinguish or suppress the emotions of sadness, hostility, and anxiety. The strategy is to not run away from or minimize your devastation or pretend that the marriage was wrong in the first place. You are standing in the truth of your pain and at the same moment you are being reborn. This rebirth is midwifed by reframing your emotions.

Everything in the universe is energy. Our thoughts are composed of electrical impulses fired by the millions of neurons in our brain. Feelings and emotions are, at their core, energy. The universe is a field of pure potential that is continually in motion. It turns out that anger, sadness, and fear, like all of our emotions, are useful. Every feeling, fully felt, creates shifts one way or another. In order for there to be healing, there must be feeling. Feelings move energy. We must move the energy so that our energy centers are clear and free-flowing.

Negative thoughts are normal and not a bad thing, for a time. In fact, these thoughts help us make judgments, have discriminating instincts, and guide us toward what is right for us and away from what is not. The process suggested in this book is not one of blind compassion, nonnegativity, or becoming a "7-Eleven around-the-clock good guy." Rather, it is one in which our answers are contained in the wisdom of self-investigation, nonreactivity, and diminishing destructive (including self-destructive) emotions.

The new emotions brought out during a divorce are usually unrecognizable, because we don't have these kinds of emotions every day. We are now experiencing emotions far more potent than everyday frustration, anxiety, and anger. When flooded with unfamiliar emotions, we fear we might drown in them. These perceptions are engendered by the erroneous fear that emotions are solid and lasting. We all love pattern and the beauty of things that last. Unfortunately, we unconsciously can believe that negative emotions last as well. Once we believe that our emotions are solid instead of fluid, we are in jeopardy of seeing the world as an unyielding and difficult place.

Developing a Passion for Compassion

We all have within us a grain of petty, ego-driven, unskillful behavior. But we also possess a lifetime of diplomacy, charity, compassion, and loyalty. All of those things combine to make up who we are. Yes, it is true that our kind, compassionate self is wrestling with our inner demons. But our goodness has not been eclipsed simply because the other part of our emotional makeup has currently become so powerful. Buddhist philosophy tells us that the sentiment that wins in the struggle between skillful and agitated behavior is the one whose seeds are watered.

Visualize yourself sitting in a chair. In that visualization, create a picture of yourself made up of only the positive things you have done with your life: the ways you have helped your friends, the way you have devoted yourself to your family, how hard you worked, and so forth. Then picture in another seat, directly across from you, a creature that is a composite of all the negative thoughts you currently have. Wouldn't that imaginary creature be much smaller? Try to carry that image with you as you go through divorce and separation, realizing that this small, snarly creature cannot be the one to take precedence over a lifetime of good work. Remembering this is an act of compassion for yourself. It may also be the beginning of recognizing that your spouse may be having exactly the same struggle. You may both be experiencing divorce as the darkening sky of a winter storm, but as long as you both share the same sky, your grief is connected.

You will be disappointed, maybe angry, and ultimately exhausted if you believe you can behave benevolently toward your spouse and immediately get reciprocal treatment. You probably know how long it takes to build trust after it has been lost. Compassion in this regard merely consists of factoring into your own pain that somebody else may be suffering as well. For example, George's wife left him because he was a workaholic in her opinion. According to her, he was too self-centered to care about her or the children. Where can you find compassion in this? Try this: "How sad that George is not able to find joy in the nonmaterial, loving relationships that a family offers. How difficult it will ultimately be for him to live a life so out of balance. Sadly, his financial absorption is so great that he is willing to go through a divorce rather than alter this behavior."

Perhaps you might consider that George is suffering as well. With this in mind, you might behave a little differently. The thing that really matters in this process, however, is how you behave, not what rewards you get for that behavior. The rewards of reciprocity may be incidental, but who you become is the essence. A compassionate interpretation of a situation offers so much more relief than a hostile one that you can almost feel your fist relax, the fist that had been clenched as a tourniquet for pain. Being kind and compassionate not because you want to be liked or treated better, but because that is who you want to be—that no one has the power to take that from you—is what matters. At first you may be kind and compassionate only because of what you are going to get out of it, but true compassion, as you will see, has no need for compensation.

Mirroring Emotions

Being in the presence of negative attitudes can be the emotional equivalent of breathing secondhand smoke. We are all part of the emotional atmosphere around us, where a give-and-take of feelings occurs regardless of what we are conscious of. In his *New York Times* article "Friends for Life: An Emerging Biology of Emotional Healing," Daniel Goleman tells us there is a class of brain cells called mirror neurons. These neurons tune into another person's internal state, including emotions, movements, and intentions, and re-create that state in our own brain. This is actually the physical chemistry of empathy. The field of science known as psychophysiology has studied couples in a relationship, including those in which there are disagreements. It has found that when one party acts with hostility and anger, the same emotional reflection or mirror image is produced in the other person, creating a habitual cellular reaction, a hooked-up circuit of negative emotions between the parties.[1]

I have watched this often in my courtroom. In one case the hostility between the former spouses was so relentless that the pickup and drop-off for the father's visitation could only take place at the child's school. Every time the parties interacted, the situation quickly deteriorated into a screaming match, further entrenching this merciless cycle. This interactive cycle was developed at the beginning of this couple's divorce, when they were at the height of their mistrust and anger. I asked myself what the payoff was in continually dragging each other to court. It became obvious that, with this negative interaction, they stayed relevant in each other lives because they still had contact. They were too vulnerable to interact without this fortress of anger, yet they could not give up the connection. They didn't realize how interrelated they were. What they did to each other they did to themselves.

Only when I told them I thought they wanted to be with each other were they embarrassed enough to look differently at their cycle of behavior. When their son started emulating his father's behavior by screaming obscenities to his mother, I could see the father realized he had gone too far. He actually felt bad for his former wife and volunteered to speak with their son. Unlike the earlier times he had been to court, I could see that recently he was feeling better about himself in the role of his former wife's rescuer. It was the first time in years that he had come closer to being true to his core values. Compassion had been one of them.

One of the things that can break this kind of negative emotional connection is compassion. I can't be sure which dynamic was at work with this father. Either he found a basis for compassion and got out of the negative cycle, or he opted out of the negative cycle and found compassion. If just one party acts with more compassion, the whole formula changes for the better. Yes, one is all it takes.

In the world of divorce, perceptions that are contaminated by fear and anger cloud the accurate assessment of the other person's emotions and fears. Paranoia, naturally, is stimulated by the reality of divorce proceedings. When we respond from those clouded emotions, we may trigger the entire cycle of hostility. In other words, through our own fear and anger, we trigger fear and anger in the mate we are dealing with. Studies on the secret of happiness reveal that if we continue in this cycle of anger, hostility, and suffering with no attempt to alter it, we suffer a small death every day. Most of us usually think of death in the large sense, as in the death of the body, but we never think of going down the wrong emotional path as a series of small soul deaths. Every choice that takes us to a higher emotional path is a small reincarnation. Every choice we make affords us the opportunity to pick what is life-enhancing or what is life-destroying.

Now, I know you are thinking: "Oh, yes, that answers the question about why I want to avoid my spouse at all costs. My spouse's terrible negativity is contagious!" If you are right, you have found your first opportunity for compassion. Compassion breaks the cycle; it acknowledges that both you and your spouse may be suffering with those negative emotions, but you have found a way out.

Many religious traditions identify compassion as one of the most sacred yearnings of the human spirit. We may say that our spouse is not worthy of our compassion or has brought on his or her own misery because of how our spouse has treated us. But compassion is our own internal work, which is not dependant upon an assessment of another's worthiness. Being compassionate releases its own set of good chemicals in our brain and actually raises self-esteem. The fact that it is contagious is an added benefit. If it appears that our spouse can only see one way to survive, and that is with hostility, then that may be a basis for compassion.

Don't Expect You or Them to Be Perfect

Skepticism is a good watchdog if you know when to take off its leash.
—Nero Wolfe, in Rex Stout's *Fer-de-Lance*

Most people want to behave kindly and have the people around them experience their goodness. All too often, though, especially in cases of divorce, we can believe one thing about ourselves and yet not act according to that belief. Such incongruence between belief and behavior breeds misery and suffering. It contributes to a feeling of being off-balance. It is difficult to sustain a clear, centered thought process when this off-balance feeling persists. I have heard it said, "If you're not actively living what you believe in, then it's not really your belief anyway." I don't agree because many forces act upon our good intentions, and those forces are magnified during the time of divorce and separation. Such forces break down trust and create great obstacles that cloud our beliefs about who we think we are and who we want to be.

By the time you are getting a divorce you may have spent many years criticizing each other. You may have become accustomed to the thought that your mate does most things wrong and doesn't even care to try to see things the way you do. Given that this may already be the mind-set, you might be tempted to tell your mate: "This doing-it-a-different-way divorce idea is not working, because you're not doing what you're supposed to do. You're not figuring this out and, as a matter of fact, you're not even trying. I am doing all the work."

The moment you make a statement like that, you have stimulated the brain center in the other person that creates anxiety about failure. Once you have stimulated your mate's brain center for anxiety, you have triggered a negative cycle. The last thing you want is more anxiety; you already have enough. You have your own roller coaster to ride; you don't have to ride your spouse's as well. The far better way of expressing your inevitable frustration might be by saying something like, "Maybe if we thought of things in this fashion," or, "Maybe there is another way of looking at this ordeal," or "I see this process a little differently." All these phrases can be executed without negative judgment and are actually reassuring. It does, however, take skill to be neutral when you are emotionally frustrated.

In a study at the University of Wisconsin, a subject was connected to a brain-imaging machine and told she was going to get a mild shock. Immediately, her anxiety level rose. The study provided a stranger to hold her hand, and the anxiety level went down. When her husband was told to hold her hand, her anxiety level went down to almost nothing.[2]

This study is one of many providing scientific proof that we are each other's "biological allies." Therefore a calm and reassuring presence on both sides really helps to ease the anxiety for both parties.

Occasionally in my courtroom I have seen divorcing parties hold hands, sit so close to each other their thighs are touching, or put an arm around one another. In those rare cases, both parties are hurt, but nevertheless try to support each other through their crisis; they strive for compassion despite their pain. But those few examples tell me that some people are able to do this. In these cases, the children inevitably fare far better. So behaving this way is not just wise and skillful, but also highly effective for the successful creation of the new, constellation family structure. These people are not waiting for the light at the end of the tunnel; for them the light is already shining.

For those of you still struggling to find compassion for your spouse, I want to emphasize the importance of keeping expectations fluid. The fact is you will have an emotional ride with extreme peaks, deep valleys, and sharp bends. Some conversations will go smoothly; others will not. I have seen cases that started amicably, and by the end of the day the husband wanted to have his wife deported—even though she was a citizen! You may be very disappointed when your experiences don't go as you had hoped. This is the process. In fact, embracing the hills and valleys—both satisfactions and disappointments—is required. Making a shift in your views has unpredictable outcomes, so it causes discomfort. It has been said that the opposite of cozy is courage.

In divorce, it is perilous to identify only one satisfactory outcome. When you argue with your spouse during a divorce dispute, the tendency is to think there can only be two outcomes—yours and the wrong one. The truth is that there is never only Scenario A or Scenario B. There are always at least C, D, and E as well.

Deep down we do have expectations about how our spouse will behave. These expectations often run like an undercurrent throughout the proceedings. As in the phrase "Hope springs eternal," on some level we all want a glimpse of that loving reaction we used to get when we had the power to effect change in our mate. Sure the marriage may be dead, but is all the love dead? Have all the fingerprints of affection been wiped clean? Nobody is a stranger to disappointment, but during divorce it takes on a heightened intensity. I once heard a husband say to his wife about their divorce when it was no longer amicable, "You ruined everything about this divorce; it could have been easy."

There is also disappointment when your spouse does not capitulate out of guilt. You expect your spouse to feel so terrible about the outcome of the marriage that opposition will be weakened. When this does not happen you suffer "spousal guilt deprivation." The expectation is that at the last moment, guilt will grab sentimentality from the jaws of greed. Calcified expectations about your encounters with your spouse, or anything else for that matter, can only create unhappiness and discouragement. Try not to project exactly how you expect negotiations to go, because if something different happens, you will be disappointed. Disappointment is, of course, part of this or any life process. You can be strong and vigorous in your negotiations; you can have a smart, tough attorney; and you can be disappointed and still feel compassion at the same time.

Rules of Engagement: Accessing and Managing Fear and Expectations

The three behavioral alternatives in the heat of divorce are fight, flight, or finding another way to relate. In my courtroom I use an exercise I created based on rules of engagement, which are usually thought of as stated policies about the use of military force. The purpose of my Rules of Engagement, however, is to reduce fear and activate communication in the absence of the parties' ability to do so. The rules are not intended to be used for the settlement of the entire case, but as a behavioral protocol during the pendency of the case. Ultimately I have used this format for settlement after the behavioral rules are in place.

In most cases you can't just approach your spouse and say, "How about a friendly divorce?" You both know a choice must be made: fight, flight, or finding another way to relate. No matter how much animosity you might feel, a fight escalates the problems (and the attorneys' fees) and is destructive if you have children. Flight is not an option that will enable you to get your needs met, and the problem will not just go away. By default perhaps you will decide to handle your divorce a different way. The Rules of Engagement are a way to start relating differently.

The rules are based on the reality that litigants have many overwhelming fears and expectations about divorce. Writing them down and presenting them to each other (usually through an attorney, but it can also be done directly) is a first step toward formulating your own Rules of Engagement. Now you each have an opportunity to suggest ways the fears can be alleviated, perhaps jointly agreeing on some issues or "trading" on others. It is an experiential exercise that shows you and your spouse what it feels like to agree, especially when you were sure you couldn't. When you get some of your intangible needs addressed, you will feel less threatened. The concept is based on the idea that if you can agree on smaller, less controversial things, the larger ones come easier. As you find out you can in fact agree, optimism is enhanced. When you start to care about the small victories you have accumulated in the earlier stages of the divorce process, you will be more reluctant to risk losing them at trial.

Wherever you are in your divorce process (just starting, in the middle of it, or even afterwards), I would suggest doing the following as soon as possible:

- Make a list of every nonfinancial fear you have about the divorce process. Include fears about how you perceive your spouse will behave, what damage you think your children will suffer from the process of divorce or the fear that you are being maligned to your friends, family, or children. Make this list extensive, but do not include financial issues at this time.

In my courtroom, I request that the list-making in the pretrial conference be done by the parties at home. I separate the financial issues from all of the rest of the items on the list and do not deal with them until I have agreements on all the nonfinancial issues. It is more effective for people to practice agreeing on the smaller, easier things first. Some of the things on the lists have been:

"Your mother hates me, and I'm afraid she will be speaking badly about me to everyone we know."

"Our child has asthma, and I don't think you are consistent with giving him his medicine."

"I am afraid that during your visitation, you will not be there and will leave the children with sitters."

"I am very concerned that I will lose all of our joint friends."

"If you give the children chocolate after nine at night, they can't sleep."

"I am afraid you will allow the children to be with your new boyfriend, and they are not ready for it."

"I am afraid the children will find your *Playboy* magazines."

I learned about the success of this effort from a couple who, according to their attorneys, despised each other. They were fighting over custody of their six-year-old son. The wife, Rebecca, who filed for divorce and sole custody, had been a stripper; during the course of the case she became a devout Pentecostal and began taking part in church activities every weekend. The husband, Armando, who had managed the strip club, was furious when Rebecca filed for divorce. In retaliation he had Rebecca's father's temporary visa revoked, and her father was sent back to his home country.

After sharing their areas of concern, they were able to begin formulating their Rules of Engagement by making small concessions. For example, they decided who would take their son to soccer games on the weekends and never to argue in front of him. They started small and found they could agree on things that seemed rather neutral. Neither had originally believed that the other was capable of being reasonable, but they each found out that their spouse could make agreements. We worked our way up to an 85 percent agreement on all the behavioral issues. On the more difficult things, like finances, the parties also started agreeing, as they were too afraid of losing at trial the gains they had already made through agreements.

After spending so many hours in this process, they were very invested in the results.

Ultimately what Armando really wanted was to have the right of first refusal with regard to parenting time with their son when Rebecca was away; that is, in Rebecca's absence, Armando wanted the option of caring for their son rather than having him stay with a third party. Even though Rebecca didn't trust him at all at the beginning of the process, she began to see that he could cooperate if they took baby steps. There is rarely a case in which people can't agree on *something*, even if one party is really resistant. Start with agreeing on the date of marriage! Rebecca, who now was in church regularly, was willing to relent on the right of first refusal. She had seen that, despite the initial viciousness Armando exhibited, he had compromised on many things.

When you want to approach your reluctant spouse about being open to the process of creating Rules of Engagement, include in your pitch the concrete realities by saying: "The choices in divorce are fight, flight, or a different way. Why don't we at least give 'a different way' a try? We can fight about the money later." Establish your Rules of Engagement first without regard to financial issues. The rules only need be concerned with the *conduct* of the parties. If you do this in the early stages, you can minimize unproductive behavior engendered by random hostility as the case goes on.

Keep the conversation about the expectations and requirements of the Rules of Engagement simple. It is just a matter of making lists and then matching for potential agreements about conduct. Tell your spouse it is an exercise to keep communication open and he or she is not obligated to settle the case with you.

As you can see, some of the items on this list may seem minor, but they are all crucial. If you sit down with your spouse to determine which items you can agree on, often with your attorneys, that is a good start. You will not be able to agree on all of them, so don't expect to. The interesting thing about the Rules of Engagement is that it is difficult for people with children to say the words, "I refuse to enter into a process that will help my children," or, "I refuse to enter into a process that attempts civility."

It will be a great comfort for your children to know that their parents have made agreements about them and about their parents' own behavior. Through this process, you two have agreed to put your children into a safety zone. This is an extraordinary way to help your children sleep at night; it helps them know that in the middle of the chaotic explosion of the life they have always known, there is a structure they can count on.

In the best-case scenario, spouses would meet once a month to see which of the agreements need to be recalibrated or whether to add or subtract different agreements. If one parent disregards the agreements, that is not a basis for the other parent to disregard them. I'm completely in favor of mediation and the collaborative-law model, and I would love to see divorcing people not use the court system as they do. In mediation, all of these agreements can be kept confidential. For those who have the advantage of working with therapists, they are a great resource to help with creating and honoring agreements.

One of the reasons the lists made for the Rules of Engagement are so useful is that people often don't know what it is that is making them so agitated and distrustful. When they write some of these fears, specifically and in detail, it is better than approaching a former partner with generalized mistrust. When people do these inventories, subconscious issues surface that would otherwise not be known.

For example, a father named Robert refused to give the mother, Beth, custody because he was afraid she would not do homework with their children. Robert and Beth entered into an agreement that if the children's homework was not done on three consecutive occasions, Robert would have the right to pick them up and do their homework with them. Once this unknown issue came to the surface and was dealt with, the case started to resolve. Robert's deep fear precluded his saying yes to a settlement at all, but he didn't know why. Education was his primary core value. Itemizing your specific needs can lead to insight on what needs are not being met and therefore why you are having a difficult time settling your case.

If you and your spouse can make some agreements about your children and your behavior, by the time you get to the negotiating table you will be more harmonious people and can bring about a more peaceful resolution. If you are furious, angry, and suspicious, without any means of reducing these emotions, there will be an entirely different outcome at the negotiating table. Some sample agreements are:

- We agree not to discuss finances in front of the children.
- When we have visitation disputes, we agree not to speak to the children about them until we first speak to each other.
- We agree that the children will only have two extracurricular activities per week, unless we both agree otherwise.
- We agree that if either of us is not going to be with the children overnight, we will give the other parent an opportunity to be with the children, even if it is on our scheduled time.
- We agree that if either parent is out of town overnight during their parenting time, the other party will have first option to be the child-care provider.

When you find yourself having a difficult time keeping your agreements, and you will, it is time to refer to your Personal Manifesto and remember the path you want to take. If you have children, a great motivator to help you stay on the path is keeping their picture with you, especially one in which they are smiling. Look at the picture and remind yourself you have the power to wipe that smile off their faces with potentially damaging behavior.

An incentive to help you maintain your agreements is the knowledge that an antagonistic separation or divorce could cost you years in the courts and endless amounts of money. Statistics show that the average divorce for middle-income families is about $30,000. For high-income families, I have seen the fees reach the millions. The average divorce traditionally takes two years to complete; I also have seen some take over four years.

If you were told that someone was going to cut an arm off one of your children, wouldn't you move heaven and earth to protect the child? And if I were to tell you that a hostile divorce amputates your children's happiness and ability to find joy or the feeling of safety for the rest of their lives, wouldn't you try to protect them? Make an agreement to make an alliance, an army of two, with your spouse, mate, or former spouse to make the children your number-one rescue mission and to do everything you can to cause them no harm. Without this army, your children are left to emotionally fend for themselves. Simply put, if karma is the result of your actions, what actions have you put in motion, and what is the fruit of your actions? The Rules of Engagement and your Personal Manifesto set the intention for good karmic action.

PART TWO

HARNESSING THE POSITIVE POWER OF NEGATIVE EMOTIONS

3

Criticism

A Flood in the Mouth, a River with No Banks

Can you remember, however vaguely, during the blissful days of your marriage, the first time you felt the cut of criticism delivered by your mate? You were probably shocked as you heard the crunch of an apple in your Garden of Eden. You had done a slow emotional striptease in front of your partner but now receive no applause and you thought you heard a "Boo" in the back row.

Hadn't you chosen your mate because this was the one person in the entire world who made you feel so good? The person you once could trust your heart to now, with the precision of a heart surgeon, had the ability and apparently the desire to cut yours out. The partner with whom you felt so secure has now woven your security blanket with broken glass.

In the beginning, we know that our mate is not perfect. But we also know that a little understanding and gentle nudging can help him or her aspire to what we believe is a better path. Of course, our mate may feel exactly the same about us. As we start to notice that our gentle nudging doesn't seem to be making a difference, we upgrade to more direct criticism. We tell ourselves we are only doing it "out of love." We say things like, "My darling, I wish you wouldn't eat so much at dinner. You know you have a blood-pressure problem, and I worry about you so." The idea that what we are saying is done "for their own good" is nothing more than an attempt to put a silk blindfold on your partner so they won't notice it is really criticism.

Criticism may start out as an act of love for many well-intentioned reasons, but like a lion cub, so cute in the beginning, it eventually becomes deadly. We have all done it; we have all felt to our core that we were trying to help our partner. After all, in marriage or a committed relationship we have hitched our wagon to our partner's. We have interlocked destinies; in essence, if our partner is harmed, we are harmed. But when we criticize, we slip into potential quicksand. Although not meant to hurt our partner in the beginning, even gently delivered criticism, after a time and with repetition, hurts and causes the recipient to become resentful. The recipient criticizes back in self-defense, and a habitual destructive pattern develops.

In a current practice, people wear a plastic bracelet on one wrist, and every time they complain, they must move the bracelet to the other wrist. The goal is to go twenty-one days without having to switch wrists. I would like to see married, separating, and divorcing people use a similar system for dealing with criticism of their partner or former partner. One of the reasons it would be difficult to do even for a day is because criticizing others serves a purpose—it relieves us from having to criticize ourselves and can be a distraction from more central issues in the relationship.

I had an experience about fifteen years ago with a strong and marvelous man named David. He was talking to me about a situation he was working through. I thought that because he was opening up to me about some personal things, it meant he was telling me: "Jump in, Michele, whenever you feel like it. Spread your opinion like peanut butter all over my personal life." After all, I thought, I have had experience and know quite a bit about the topic. After I made some comments, he gently but strongly said to me, "I know you have a lot to say, and I think you are very smart, but when I want your opinion, I will ask for it." I learned then that it is not merely a matter of being right or having knowledge; criticism is effective only when you are invited to give it.

As a result of that conversation, which at the time hurt my feelings, my relations with everyone seemed to improve. Most important, when my son turned eighteen I said to him: "You know that I have an opinion about everything you do, but I am not going to volunteer. Anytime you want it, you just have to ask." To this day we converse freely, asking for and giving each other advice, which may include its close cousin criticism, if requested.

"I did it for her own good." Think about this: Isn't most criticism done under the guise of being for someone else's betterment? After all, criticism is not the same thing, and supposedly does not have the same motivation, as an insult. In my opinion, uninvited criticism feels to the receiver like an insult. If you don't agree, think back to the last time you were criticized, how you felt—which part of that was "good"? In relationships, most of us love to mold the behavior and the reactions of our mates so they can start to become who we need them to be. Criticism is the sculpting knife we use in our attempt to create the person we want. Often I have chewed the side of my mouth just to keep from blurting out the little nugget that in my mind would solve my mate's problem.

For example, if my partner got angry with his son and I thought he was being too harsh, would it be advisable for me to say so? My partner and his son have issues to work out that are strictly between them. My partner's anger might be justifiable, important for his son to hear, and carry a weight that might get his son's attention and inspire him to be responsible and accountable. But if I offer my opinion uninvited, I may anger my partner and derail him and his son from the path they are on. Am I to say nothing? No. I might say, "I would like to help you with your distress concerning your son, if you would like me to." Or, "I am sorry your son is having such a hard time. Do you feel like talking about it?" Or, "Do you ever think that a third party, like a therapist, just for a couple of sessions, would help your son? Or you?"

I have a girlfriend who has beautiful red hair and loves to wear her burgundy dress. She wears it often, and in my opinion it is not flattering. If I criticize her burgundy dress, I may be interfering with her positive energy and the intention she had when she put it on. Without an invitation for my opinion, I am disrupting and eroding her positive emotions. Her good feelings are sacrificed to my need to make the point, even though I think I am helping. If she asks me, "How does this dress look on me?" then I have been invited to give an opinion.

Divorce: A Buffet of Criticism, All You Can Eat!

When there is separation and divorce, trust is shifting like the ground in an earthquake; you are giving and receiving avalanches of criticism. You remember well the day you were thrown a medicine ball of unforgivable criticism; it hit you in the stomach and you finally said, "No more!" It was the first time you allowed the reality that your relationship was ending to settle upon you. Now even a compliment is looked at suspiciously. "You really look nice today," or, "I like your haircut," to you now means he is looking for a better settlement. "Have a nice day at work," or, "That suit looks good on you," makes you think this is the day she is going to clear the furniture out of the house. The stage on which you play out your last days together as a couple is painted with the patina of mistrust, and even an innocent suggestion is viewed as having an ulterior motive behind it.

You have moved to the irritation zone, where a compliment given to you by your partner causes displeasure. "I like the way you handled the situation with our neighbor. That was very diplomatic," causes you to ask: "Why didn't she ever say that before? Is she saying it because she's up to something, or is this compliment a prelude to an insult rather than a kiss?" In the irritation zone you try to pretend normalcy, but almost everything your partner says buzzes around your ears like a fly you want to swat.

When people decide to separate, they believe they are finally getting away from what clearly has been an overdose of criticism. I have seen such hypersensitivity in court among separating and divorcing people that a comment such as, "Yes, I admit he's a pretty good father," is met with the response, "Why didn't you ever say that before? It takes a judge and a courtroom to pull that out of you?" I've seen people in court, and my own friends who are going through separation, reject people who might help them if they so much as smell the aroma of criticism. At this point the ability to sort out unjustified comments from valuable feedback has been lost. Although they are most sensitive to their soon-to-be former spouse, much valuable information from lawyers, friends, and therapists is rejected because it hits the criticism nerve.

In a recent case a woman insisted on coming into court to get her ap-pliances—toaster, microwave, blender, and so on—out of the house. Her lawyer told her she was being petty and unreasonable. She fired him on the spot. He was only trying to save her money on legal fees, because she would be able to obtain those appliances in a few months anyway, and it would cost her thousands of dollars to go to court now for the property. But his criticism hit that nerve, and a warning alarm went off. When her system registered "enemy," her ability to filter the information effectively shut down. She was now on the road to associating only with friends, law-yers, and others who thought the way she did and agreed with her.

I had a good friend who had been criticized endlessly by his wife for thirty years. By the time they separated, he had what I call in my court "criticized spouse repetition syndrome" (CSRS). Under his calm but raw surface he had kerosene running through his veins. He was vulnerable to anyone striking a match of criticism. If you so much as suggested that his wife might have made a rational point, he would not only ignite, but blow up the friendship.

Many of us have finely tuned the mechanism that screens out help-ful suggestions if they have any critical content. Unfortunately, when going through a divorce or separation we are not at our best—we are vulnerable, and much of our behavior is unskillful. This is a time when kind, loving direction may be desperately needed—and a time when it is often rejected. For example, your best friend tells us that after you speak to your wife, you become short-tempered with your children. Your immediate response may be, "You don't support me," or, "You're on her side." Sometimes when our former spouse criticizes us, we may know there is some truth in it, but it is hard to take criticism from someone we no longer trust. Although criticism is often interpreted negatively, it may be valuable. When we have endured years of criti-cism and have had to practice blocking it out, our blocking mechanism works so well that we start rejecting even helpful advice.

During our divorce it appears we have been granted a hunting li-cense for shooting arrows of criticism at our partner. Even more than that, we ruminate about his or her bad qualities and itemize incorrect behavior to bolster our position and justify the end of the marriage. But in doing this we can lose so much. Giving criticism, like taking anabolic steroids, makes us feel strong and keeps us on our path to leave the relationship or minimize the loss. But steroids provide a false energy that leaves us weaker when we stop using them.

The Critic in the Courtroom: "That's My Story and I'm Sticking to It"

The person who has always referred to you as "my darling" is now speaking about you in court as if he or she was a reporter for the *National Enquirer*. Suddenly, your parenting skills border treacherously on child abuse. Criticism of your mate has become a frequent-flier program: the more you criticize, the more bonus points you rack up during the separation or divorce. The perception is that the more you criticize, the more mileage you will get in court, and that the more vulnerable to criticism your partner is, the less you are.

For example, Charlie gambled away a sizable amount of his and his wife's assets. His wife, Annie, disliked Charlie's children from a previous marriage and rarely invited them to the couple's house. By the time the case got to court, Charlie's story line was that their marriage broke apart because Annie didn't get along with his children. Annie's story line was that their marriage broke apart because of Charlie's gambling.

Criticisms form the building blocks of our story line. The story line created by Annie also included: "My husband gambled. He was irresponsible, and he really didn't care about taking care of the family. He didn't care that I might need money. He stayed out late and didn't call. I would find gambling receipts in his pocket, and he would lie about them."

A story line becomes a fortress we use to protect ourselves. But as with all fortresses, there are structures in place to control the things that go out and come in. As you can see, Annie's story line leaves out the part where she might be accountable or even at fault. Thus complete truth in this example is barricaded out for the sake of holding on to the story line. Building a fortress of ideas about separation or divorce requires us to compartmentalize information. Part of us knows the whole truth, but needs to suppress it. When we become adept at suppressing truth, it is not limited to just one situation. That mechanism, that ability to compartmentalize, makes it possible to eliminate the whole truth whenever necessary or convenient.

For example, in a custody fight you might believe it is crucial to focus only on your former partner's bad behavior and forget all the good parenting, like those many long nights when he was working so hard to get your daughter's fever down. But experience mixed with emotions makes up the compost that nourishes wisdom and enlightenment. To seal off any one of those components from the others takes enormous, unconscious energy. And if we do not allow ourselves to embrace the whole truth of our separation or divorce, then we cannot learn the real lessons.

So, for example, in the case of Annie and Charlie above, she will believe that her lesson is to not get involved with anyone who gambles, or with anyone who doesn't have well-buttoned-downed spending habits. Maybe an accountant would be her ideal mate. Where is the truth and lesson in that? She has wrapped herself tightly in partial truth and therefore cannot scroll down to the pay dirt. Annie needs to consider: Why did she choose someone who was likely to disappoint her? Why did she feel competitive with her stepchildren? Why did she choose to not get help together with Charlie? Without the insight into what she needs to address after the divorce is over, she may believe the marriage ended solely because of Charlie's reckless money habits. (I wouldn't be surprised to find her all dressed up and hanging out at H&R Block trying to date an accountant.)

Two psychologists, John Gottman and Robert Levenson, did a study examining seventy-three married couples. By listening for ten minutes to how they spoke to one another, they were able to predict which marriages would survive. Among other things, the researchers asked each couple to discuss a problem area or topic of continuing disagreement in the marriage. Later they determined the ratio of criticisms to compliments in the couples' discussions. The more a husband and wife turned to criticism rather than complimentary statements during a debate or argument, the more likely the marriages were doomed to fail.[1]

One example they use was an argument about whether a couple should get a dog. The dialogue of the more critical couple was along these lines: "You know you never will walk the dog. You know I'm going to end up walking it. I always end up taking care of things you don't finish." A line from the couple predicted to have greater marital success went more like this: "I know you are very nurturing and so good with animals, but at this point it's too much responsibility for either of us." This study illustrates the crucial role that criticism can play in any interaction, whether it is within a continuing marriage or relationship or one that is breaking up.

If you have to say something and are intent on getting a point across—and not just for the sake of being critical—you might add a compliment to your criticism:

> After your former spouse is late with the children again you might say: "You brought the children home late because you took Lake Shore Drive and it was crowded? I suppose that is a more scenic ride for the children, and I know you wanted to show them the boats, but that makes me late for my next appointment."

> "I asked you not to let the children watch R-rated movies. I guess you believe they are more mature than I do, because you are good at giving them the benefit of the doubt, but we definitely disagree on that."

> "I know you are short-tempered, but I noticed you were more patient with the children than usual. That's really great."

> "How could you allow your lawyer to yell at me in court? It's not like you to let somebody talk to me that way, and it's not your nature to be nasty."

Criticism Deflectors

No suggestion works every time, but here are some considerations when you want to be on a more skilled path with yourself, your children, or your former partner:

1. After you have been criticized you might say: "You may have a point. I would like to think about it, and we can discuss it later in the week," or, "Let me think about what you said, and let's make an appointment to discuss it, but not in front of the children." This validates the possibility that your former spouse might have a point while cooling the

flames for both of you, giving you both the time to think about what you want to say and protecting the children. Children learn how to criticize and how to react to criticism from their parents.

2. Before the discussion escalates into an argument, you might say, "I know I frustrate you, and I appreciate your efforts to be less critical."

3. After you have been criticized you might say, "It feels like you are being really critical of me, but I'm not in a mood to take it personally." (That statement is a little devilish, as it really frustrates the criticizer.)

4. Remember, you are not the warden of your former spouse's behavior, so you don't have to scold, lecture, or sound like a disciplinarian.

5. Not reacting defensively can be very empowering; you have found the power to allow others to be wrong. Allow yourself the freedom to not be the one chosen to instruct them in their misguided ways.

6. Tone—on the phone, in the home, or in a neutral zone—makes or breaks the effect. Say this statement nicely: "You were always a very loving, generous husband." Now say the same statement sarcastically. You get the picture.

7. After you have been criticized, ask yourself if it is possible that there is even a kernel of truth in what was said. Don't do this during the conversation—it's a reflective exercise for later and needs a calm mental space to be effective. When I feel criticized, I hear a bugle call summoning all my soldiers to begin the battle cry: "Why I am right and you are wrong." If someone criticizes me, I want an immediate divorce, even if I am not married to him. This is not the time to engage in serious self-reflection. *Later*, as an exercise, make a list of any things you might learn from the criticism.

If your goal is to get your needs met, it is not hard to see the sabotaging effects of criticism. It is the spoiler of all communication. When communication breaks down, there is risk of real anger, as there is no language left to diffuse it. In the next chapter we consider sources of anger other than criticism. You can learn not to criticize, but it is harder to learn to reduce anger. I will show you how it can be done, for your benefit.

4

The Stains of Heartbreak

Hot-, Warm-, or Cold-Blooded Anger

Anger is the garbage of all emotion, but it takes garbage to
make compost, and it takes compost to make a flower.
—THICH NHAT HANH

ou never could have known that the fate of your marriage was being cast at the same time you walked down the aisle on your wedding day. The sanctuary created by marriage insulated you from your most primal fears: abandonment, danger, even insecurities about food and shelter. Now that all seems like an illusion, and by the time you separate from your spouse, you don't know which part was fantasy and which was real. You tell yourself that if it were real love, estrangement could have never happened. You ask yourself whether you should have seen it was a mistake from the beginning. You want to believe that, no matter what flaws have been revealed over the years and even though you are headed for divorce, the one you married still has some tenderness for you. But when that hope melts away . . .

Anger is the harvest of failed expectations. When we love someone we don't expect that person to cause devastation in our lives. We expect that our love will be the one who, above everyone else, will protect us. No matter what the divorce rate is, we believe we can be one of the exceptions. Up until the end, we want the marriage we have dreamed of to be sustained. The greater the disappointment we experience, the higher the bonfire of fury rises. Anger now enhances our sense of "otherness," obliterating the former rose-colored illusions of "being one."

No matter what the reason, no matter how you allocate the fault, in the end it feels like betrayal of vows and promises. You don't have to resurrect Freud to see why you might be furious. In spite of divorce statistics, you still feel that your situation is unique and your pain singular. If you have children, there is the bond of having created a family, and you know you may never have another experience that equals the moment you two looked at your firstborn child together for the first time. It seems too hard to simply reduce affection for your spouse; it seems much easier to go completely in the other direction, that of anger and hate.

It would be logical to assume that by the time separation occurs, you no longer expect anything from your mate—except possibly the worst. Surprisingly, I have found that in divorce people develop a renewed and heightened state of expectation, as they believe their spouse's remorse will create more benevolence. The vows are still remembered on some level, even if unconsciously. After all, the attachment is still there and has yet to be fully dismantled. Often there is a perception on the part of at least one spouse that the other person should feel guilty for his or her part in the disintegration of the marriage and should be more yielding and repentant.

The Purpose of Anger

It appears that your world is falling apart, and you can no longer predict anything about your life, the actions of your spouse, or the intense emotions of your children. You are vulnerable to your attorneys and to the unpredictable legal system; understandably you feel lost and completely powerless over your experiences and emotions. It is all you can do just to protect yourself from what feel like daily attacks by everyone around you. You can't even be sure that your own emotions won't ambush you as you react to the injustices that seem to compound every day.

The emotion that masquerades as power and counteracts this feeling of powerlessness better than any I know is anger. This emotional pharmaceutical masks the pain while simultaneously producing an endless supply of energy. It feels better to be enraged than impotent. Although it later shows itself to be an imposter, the feeling of power we derive from anger is irresistibly seductive. Real power comes with wisdom and an understanding of the source of our fears, but when wisdom and insight seem unavailable, the deceptive power of anger substitutes for them.

Imagine if your emotions had no built-in alarm system, if you could be injured or insulted and not even know it. You would have no ability to protect yourself. Anger says, "You cannot do that to me!" It is the invisible electric fence that, when crossed, sends a signal of violation. It is a call to action. Anger serves the purpose of triggering the fight-or-flight response for self-protection and survival.

However, when you are enmeshed in divorce, flight is not an option, and you feel you are caught in the jaws of some terrible force. In fact, one of the more hellish aspects of divorce is that it seems as though it is never going to end. You may think fighting is your only available option. Many people believe that the only fuel for a fight is anger—that you have to be angry to be able to fight and therefore protect yourself.

Unique features in a divorce stimulate vigorous emotional reactions. You are suddenly no longer being validated for all the good you have done in the marriage. The emotional, financial, and physical investments you have made in your marriage have been marked down to a value of zero. You float on a sea of troubling injustice and misunderstanding, as over and over again you are unfairly characterized by your spouse, the other attorney, or the judge. You ache with the pain of being portrayed in a negative or false light you believe you don't deserve; you feel devalued, blamed, not trusted. Whatever triggers it, your anger serves a purpose in helping you realize the values you wish were recognized.

The Causes of Anger

The causes of anger are many and can stem directly from the divorce process. Sometimes anger arises out of primitive instinct, and sometimes as a reaction to true wrong or injustice. Other times anger occurs when there are assaults on self-perception or ego. The interesting thing at this level is that anger is not the primary emotion. Although it is the most outward manifestation of our emotional state, the underlying emotion is sadness, often accompanied by fear and frustration.

The more primitive motivators may include the following:

- If shelter is jeopardized, fear is engendered because the survival instinct is activated.
- Perceived potential harm to children activates fear in the parent.
- Interference with access to one's children activates fear of losing the children.
- Facing survival without a job after having given up a career to raise a family galvanizes fear for the stay-at-home parent.
- When there is loss of trust, a spouse can no longer be relied on to get needs met, which stimulates fear and dread.
- In ancient times leaving a tribe was a death sentence via starvation or physical danger. Today, some may have an almost archetypal fear that divorce will exclude them from a "tribe"—a beloved family they entered through marriage.

Some recurrent secondary sources that inspire anger are more specific and immediately provocative. These include, among others:

- Sexual betrayal
- Hiding money
- Your spouse's "barracuda" attorney who has clear orders to destroy you
- Lying, about anything

Anger that arises from reasons of the ego or diminished self-esteem:

- Fear of failure, not living up to the expectations of society
- Fear of being taken advantage of
- Preoccupation with winning

- Not being vindicated as "a good person" by the court
- No longer getting any attention
- Feeling exploited (e.g., "You don't care for me at all; now it's all about money")
- Being wrongly blamed (your perception)
- Not being allowed to be the rescuer of a mate
- Self-criticism because we created an illusion of our spouse that was not who they really were.

This is a partial list, for example only. There are hundreds of pieces to this puzzle, and any combination of them can trigger anger. And if that isn't enough, consider the impact of years of resentments that have built up from the bottled-up anger that has yet to explode.

It is immeasurably better to look anger in the face than to have its detrimental effects stab us in the back. Because anger is a symptom of fear and pain, unless we know our diagnosis, we can't find the right medicine. If we live with anger all the time, it can be dangerous, because, as they say, people who live on the seashore can't hear the waves. The key is not to adapt to or even overindulge in an anger-driven existence, but to identify the source of the anger. One day we wake up and want to create a better life and don't know where to start. It has become difficult to diffuse our anger, because we can no longer track its real source. The waves of anger have washed away the footprints in the sand.

A Lifetime of Anger Finally Takes Center Stage

Consider how much more you often suffer from your anger and grief, than from those very things for which you are angry and grieved.
—Marcus Antonius

We may have spent a lifetime suppressing our anger in a relationship in which our unwritten contract would not allow its release or expression. The contract terms may have been that, in order for us to get our needs met, we had to take a vow of silence. Many of us do this and later feel enslaved and then accustomed to absorbing our anger and letting it sit in our cells. This comes to an abrupt and screeching halt when divorce agitates past resentments with brutal force. One way or another, anger at past wrongs will come spewing out like a shaken Pepsi.

This may be the first opportunity not only to access those emotions, but to express them as well. We may have, for the first time, a mouthpiece—our lawyer. This is why in my courtroom I often see anger that seems out of proportion to the generating offense. This historical anger is hyperdestructive; it has an enhanced charge that is difficult to locate or analyze because it has existed for so long. This entrenched anger is often expressed in ways that are inappropriate and make it difficult to deconstruct. If you don't know what it is, it is hard to fix.

In my courtroom, some litigants believe that acting out their anger will provide an emotional release, perhaps a release for which they have waited many years. Many divorcing people believe their anger can be relieved by a surrogate—their attorney. But I have yet to see couples who take a hostile approach to one another find any relief as the case progresses. One case that ultimately resulted in disaster occurred because the stepfather wanted more visitation with his stepson. Under the law of Illinois he had no rights to visitation at all. His wife, the mother, was letting him see the child once a week, but the stepfather wanted to see him more. He had supported the child for six years before his wife moved out without any warning. He then hired the toughest attorney he could find. She was so aggressive and hostile to the mother that the mother terminated all contact between her child and the stepfather. He could have slowed his attorney down, but his angry mind was getting satisfaction from the misguided sense of power his attorney gave him.

Anger's amphetamine-like effect masquerades as a powerful surge of energy. It increases confidence and motivation and for a time induces a false sense of power. When someone violates our deepest values, it triggers our sense of righteous anger. Empowered by anger, we are also able to resist giving in to sadness. As anger releases adrenaline into our system, we are no longer sad and sluggish, but motivated into action. Practically speaking, anger is the default emotion that prevents us from feeling weak. We all know how inarticulate we can become when we are angry. Our pulse races, and we feel we must do something. When this is our mental state, we can't say what we really mean. We say more than we want to, and we say it with a mean spirit. Ambrose Bierce, the journalist and short-story author, captured it when he said, "Speak when you are angry and you will make the best speech you will ever regret."

A surge of anger gets people's attention and can be intimidating. It is a muscular cover for fear, sadness, or weakness that appears to carry dominance. It can motivate you to not only take a position, but to do all the follow-up work that is required. It shows the opposing attorney, your attorney, and your spouse that you are not a pushover. Yes, this all works for a while, but it has short-term durability, and like a snort of cocaine the price is very high.

Crime Scene Investigation: Who Is to Blame?

The impulse to blame is firmly grounded in our biology. It comes from our limbic system, the primitive brain that is fully developed by age three. (The problem-solving part of our brain, the neocortex, is not fully developed until age twenty-five.) The primitive limbic system cannot wait to lay blame. This is an automatic response forged long before our thinking brain developed the ability to cultivate thought and use logic. During a divorce we are not inspired to do any of this cultivation. We blame, reactivating past injuries, which is emotionally satisfying at first. Problem solving, which entails the effort to work through challenging issues in the present and future, is much less fun.

But consider the outcomes. Blaming locks us into a mode whose primary focus is the determination of fault and the allocation of guilt. Blame puts us in the penalizing mode, not the resolution mode. It is impossible to blame and resolve simultaneously. If we choose blame as the focus, and do so repeatedly, we become progressively more powerless. The law of diminishing returns is in full operation at this point, and soon more and more blaming is needed to fortify our position.

We sometimes use blame to minimize guilt and justify our own conduct. We find the other person to be at fault and then adhere to that belief, so guilt will not seep in. There are much better ways to alleviate guilt that might really address the problem, such as making apologies or amends, but we will never do them, once we have shifted the blame to the other person. When we blame another, we forfeit an authentic opportunity to reduce our own guilt in a sustaining way.

If you go into your next relationship believing your spouse is to blame, what have you learned that you can take with you? After all you have been through, you may end up concluding that all those of that gender are to blame. If you have not taken any responsibility, you can't change or enhance your personal development and find your way to peace and happiness. Blame shifting takes less effort, but never serves you.

An odd fact of biology is that only humans develop resentment toward others. It is possible to make animals mad, but you can't make them resentful. Resentment, the practice of holding on to blame and anger, is a subconsciously purposeful strategy for protection of the ego. Resentment can make us myopic in our view of an offense by continuously stimulating the original negative feeling. As William H. Walton put it, "To carry a grudge is like being stung to death by one bee." In a hardened state of resentment, we no longer allow alternative interpretations. In its most extreme state, resentment damns eternally, even for a minor offense. Any good that the offender has done in the past becomes muffled by our resentment. When this takes hold, redemption is not possible for the object of our scorn, as we continue to gather information that will reinforce a perspective that excludes all other views. The viciousness of resentment comes full circle when the offender begins to develop resentment toward us in response to our unforgiving stance.

Once a cycle of resentment is formed between two former loved ones, they are locked in a ghastly psychic waltz. The music is a broken record, and they spend excessive time circling meaninglessly in a shared and empty mental ballroom, thick with the dust and grime of recrimination and bitterness. As in a *Twilight Zone* episode, time stops and so does learning, as the grim and silent dancers glare at one another across the years.

But people do move on with their lives. They meet other lovers, remarry, find happiness. Although life may appear to move on in the

physical sense, in the realm of the emotional unresolved anger and resentment do not totally evaporate. Even if forced underground by the
sheer determination of our will, the polluted, noxious river of anger
continues to flow beneath the surface. This is why we use denial—we are
in serious need of an amnesiac. Retreating into our primitive brains,
we figure, "Hey, if you can't get rid of the bad feeling, hide it so you
won't have to experience it anymore." Ultimately, however, denial is an
ineffective vehicle for attaining wisdom, because learning, which will
really empower us and help eliminate future pain, is blocked.

Although anger can be explosive, resentment is a steady rhythmic
undercurrent that can reach up, attach to, and pull into itself issues
that may have nothing to do with what initially created it. In this mind-
set, nothing is too trivial to be beyond the current's reach.

I had a case in which the father was careless with the administration of medicine for the parties' eight-year-old daughter. The mother
went ballistic, because it activated all her anger systems, especially the
one for protecting her child. She denounced his parenting, proclaimed
the child in danger with him, and predicted (for good measure) that
not just the child, but anyone who came in contact with him, would get
hurt. The picture she painted was clear. Attila the Hun and Saddam
Hussein paled in comparison.

You see—although she didn't—there is an appropriate middle
ground between rational disagreement and verbal blast. You can explode, if you cannot resist, and not be abusive or vicious. Had I scripted
that mother, instead of saying, "You always do it wrong. You don't care
about our daughter. You are too busy watching TV. You are hurting our
daughter," she would have said, "I am furious. This medicine is vital
to our child's health. It is dangerous to miss a dose or to take it at the
wrong interval. It frightens me, and I don't trust you when this happens. Is there any explanation you want me to listen to?"

This well-intentioned and frightened mother torpedoed her own
case with exaggeration stimulated by fury. The child was not in danger
all the time, and not everyone who came in contact with the father got
hurt. He was undoubtedly not perfect, but what she said could not
possibly have been true. By her overstatement she lost credibility,
which appeared to be washed away by her venom. In her zeal to protect

her child, the mother destroyed her chance to deal with her spouse in a way that would promote getting her needs met.

I accept the obvious. As a divorcing couple, you are in a pressure cooker. The only pressure valve apparent to you may be to inflict pain on each other. Maybe you want to change one another's behavior. Perhaps you need release for your frustration or just acknowledgment that the other party has done wrong. The problem is you want it all *now*. But you can't have it all now, and you know it.

You have raged before, and even though in the moment it holds the promise of relief, you know it turns out badly—badly for everybody, but especially for you. At the first moments of your anger, you may feel you have just been injected with truth serum and are now possessed with an imperative to lay everything on the line and "tell it like it is." The fact that this may destroy a lifetime of intimacy, trust, and camaraderie between you, your mate, and your children may not dissuade you from your suicide mission.

Your lack of anger control is rendered even more deadly by your knowledge of the target. As a spouse, you know better than anyone on earth how best to reach that most vulnerable soft spot, or worse, hot spot: you can smell the toast when it burns. You know exactly where all the old aches and pains reside, and you have a doctorate in the geography of your spouse's childhood disappointments. With precision, you go right to the heart of the pain, and you do it effortlessly.

With my alternative approach, even though you are angry, you still allow the other person to take a position. This allows for communication rather than assassination. Communication creates potential for change, both in the other person's behavior and in your perception of it. By allowing your spouse to respond with "another explanation," he or she doesn't feel caged or trapped in your anger. And you don't have to be trapped in your anger either. You have now accommodated both your raging emotions and also the other person's ability to respond. You have indicated you are willing to listen while still maintaining the right to be angry. Considering that life includes struggle, why would we expect there not to be as much volatility in relationships? The need to communicate displeasure is still honored; you don't have to suppress it, nor does it have to get out of control.

With a little compassion for yourself, you would create a space between the crescendo and the waning of your anger. In that space you will have reduced the anger chemical load, and although you may not have changed your mind, you will certainly have changed your delivery. Not reacting when triggered and creating that space before reacting are easier said than done. The eighth-century Indian monk Shantideva refers to it as reframing your attitude toward discomfort, which you begin to do by just sitting in that angry feeling without the need to do something about it immediately. The more you repeat an explosive reaction, the more you strengthen that reaction; you strengthen the neuropathways, so that they speed you to that negative reaction faster and more often. The more often you react in anger or resentment, the more heightened your susceptibility is to different irritations and eventually even to minor ones. If that is your attitude of choice, other attitudes such as peace or happiness have no room to flourish.

Each time you cause someone harm, you may very well be picking up a little karmic debt you don't want to have to repay. This is not a bad motivation for creating that space. In that space you can watch your behavior and say to yourself, "Yes, I can be easily provoked by my spouse. I can see that." When you look objectively at your anger this way, you have found the ability to uncover your strength that lies beneath the surface. That is where power is. You can do that anytime you are ready, no matter how you have reacted before. Who knows when you will be ready to make this shift. Your power is just waiting there to be called upon.

Chain-Smoking the Offense: Ruminating

Although raging anger is not permanent, when residual anger becomes fixed you can be in real trouble. If you have been offended, how much do you ruminate about the insult? Novelist George Eliot captured the sentiment perfectly when she said, "Anger and jealousy can no more bear to lose sight of their objects than love." Ruminating is essential when you are deeply committed to holding on to a negative thought pattern. Thoughts that do not take into account another perspective cannot be 100 percent accurate. Ruminating helps us reinforce the desired version in our consciousness, while we continue to collect evidence to support it. By continuing to reheat our resentments, we can embroider the story any way we want.

It becomes clear that whether you are right or wrong is not the issue, as you can, over time and with practice, make yourself believe you are right. But this negative repetition can harm you more than your spouse could ever have. In your steady stream of negative contemplation, you have probably convinced yourself, whether it's true or not, that your spouse intended to harm you. But if you expand your rumination to include the notion that your spouse may have insulted you because he or she is in horrible turmoil and desperately afraid, you can pierce the tough skin of that original thought. Could any of your spouse's defenses have validity? If any of them is a little bit true, doesn't that reframe your I-have-been-injured story line? If you can reframe that story line, you will not need to ruminate about it as much, because it will have lost intensity. Repetition creates perceptual habits that obstruct wisdom. It can never benefit you to let your mind put up the bars of its own prison, one damaging thought at a time.

Scientists agree that the brain centers are stimulated whether there is an actual situation or just the thought of that situation. A worrisome, fearful thought means "I am in danger," and the brain responds as if something dangerous is actually happening: The heart beats faster, the muscles contract, breathing becomes rapid. If a negative or angry thought has no outlet, it feeds back into the mind and creates an even more anxious thought.

Bestselling spiritual author Eckhart Tolle talks about toxic energy interfering with the harmonious function of the body, saying, "The food it requires to replenish itself consists of energy that is compatible with its own, which is to say energy that vibrates at a similar frequency." The injuring party depends for sustenance on the recipient's reacting in pain. When the recipient no longer reacts with the same pain (change of attitude), the offender no longer has the same experience of satisfaction. Stimulating the anger becomes important for the cycle to continue, because the parties' brains are now used to being fed by this negative stimulation. On the other hand, if one of the two has strong composure, compassion, or just a sense of humor about the event, that cycle can be broken.

Scientists have found that by reinforcing negative thoughts, brain maps can enlarge their receptive field and represent more of the body's surface, increasing pain sensitivity. Pain signals in one brain map can spill into an adjacent map and develop into referred pain. Physically, referred pain is when we are hurt in one part of the body, but the pain is felt in another. The same can be true of emotional pain, which of course includes the splattering emotion of anger.

Reducing or reframing anger creates positive bonds that seem to trigger neuroplastic change by unlearning and dissolving negative neuronal networks. The part of our brain that controls emotions and relationships has the same plasticity as other parts of our brain. When we change our attitude about our anger, different neurons will fire in the brain, upgrading our brain chemistry, its function, and vitality.

The Price of Anger

Sustained anger as a mode for managing fear will wear you out. The more you use anger to try to destroy the opposition, the more tired you become. You will be so occupied in this heightened state that eventually it will be difficult to remember how to get relief. Well-practiced anger ignores other ways of responding. I have seen people self-destruct rather than risk letting anyone else destroy them. Researchers at the University of North Carolina have found that people who have antagonistic hostility that is expressed angrily, either verbally or physically, are likely to have high levels of cholesterol. They found that men and women with higher levels of hostility also showed higher levels of homocystine in the blood, which is strongly associated with heart disease.[2]

Psychologists studying the reaction of our bodies during anger found that physical symptoms occur during the stages of rage, when our bodies are flooded with adrenaline. Some of the physical problems include heart disease, increase in blood pressure, and constriction of blood vessels in the digestive track. During this phase we are often closed to any advice or reasonable interpretation that contradicts our view. Even a false feeling of power can seem better than feeling devalued or sad. I am sure you can remember the last time you were angry with your spouse and called a friend, ostensibly for advice. If your friend reacted logically, suggesting you give your spouse the benefit of the doubt, you may well have been ready to ship your friend out on the next boat. You just weren't ready to listen to logic. At such a point, all we can do is dump our emotional debris on the unwitting listener.

We may even ask ourselves, "Why can't I seem to stop or shut up when I'm angry?" There have been times when I have been willing to risk everything, because I needed to say what was on my mind. A small voice in my head said, "Don't say it. Just don't say it," but I was unable to stop. The surge of adrenaline accompanying anger was so great that I felt I was on top of a mountain and the hills were alive with the sound of my truth. Such a behavioral imperative is not simply words running off the track of reason. In this state, we are overcome by a tidal wave of chemicals flooding our body. The chemicals are actually doing the talking at such times; while our brains take a backseat, our run-amok chemistry drives the car. This chemical wave tells us we will feel release if we unleash the venom. Inevitably we are surprised when the venom comes back like a boomerang. In his book *Why Zebras Don't Get Ulcers*, Robert Sapolsky says that anger chemicals, cortisol and glucocorticoids, are destructive if they remain in the human body for an extended period. They can, over time, impair the function of the immune and endocrine systems.[3]

Even though the side effects of anger may be devastating, many of us use it as the drug of choice. When anger is allowed ascendancy, we forfeit our ability to remember any of the good times during our marriage. In the same way we find it hard today to remember life before cell phones, we now have forgotten the times we and our spouse were partnered against the world's strife, when we shared goals, hopes, and visions. The beautiful memories that are the benchmarks of our life together have slipped away like a diamond ring falling into the garbage disposal. Anger has flipped the switch, turning sweet memory into indistinguishable sewage.

Successful mourning of a marriage does not have to result in cor-ruption of memory. Even though we suffer phantom pain from the loss of our spouse in our heart, we don't have to finish cutting the ties by killing good memory. When we are devoted to killing memory using angry thoughts, we attach to dead tissue and cannot find the marriage's redeeming usefulness. We need living tissue to nourish our future life. Living tissue is found by bridging the positive aspects of our history into our future life.

When good memories are lost, it is almost impossible to germinate the potent seeds planted during our time together and to re-create a new postdivorce world based on all of its past strengths. What we have left is arid soil, watered only by acid rain. It is all too easy to lose the sense of meaning in your life, potentially converting it from "We had so much good together," to, "I wasted ten years with that person."

Anger takes too much focus and energy. Sustaining anger re-quires continually shining a spotlight on its target, leaving little time for other goals, such as moving on into the future. When you feed that anger, you nourish a twisted limb, and the result is twisted healing. To heal the limb takes work, and it will not heal straight if left to chance. In other words, you can't act any way you want, be rough on yourself and others just to get through, and expect no consequences.

One of my cases, sadly, exemplified the futility of this misdirected energy. The husband and wife owned seven apartment complexes. The husband, who managed them, let all the properties go into disrepair during the divorce, and the apartments became difficult to rent. He felt he had done all the work, and if his wife didn't want to be married to him, he would be "damn sure" she would not get any of the profits from his labor. Essentially he was saying that he didn't care what price he had to pay to make sure she was unhappy. He bragged to me that in his grief process he had finally moved to the anger stage. The problem is he lingered there too long. By the end of the case he filed for bank-ruptcy.

If you are laden with anger, you will not only compromise healing; you will be blind to the hand of fate. An important event or lesson could be happening before your eyes, but because of the intense focus that anger requires, you might miss it. When anger blankets the broken heart, it is hard for the healing energy to penetrate, and pain remains for years after the divorce. Anger cannot heal the heart; healing the heart takes a different kind of attention.

Diffusing Anger: Miraculous Things Can Happen in the Mud

When you notice yourself feeling angry, ask yourself this question: Are you more committed to self-knowledge and wisdom than to being right? We are all multifaceted: sometimes we are right, sometimes wrong, and sometimes a mixture; occasionally we overreact or underreact. There can be no objective standard of perfection—we are all contradictory and inconsistent. We have all been illogical, hypocritical, paradoxical, and unpredictable. It is part of the nature of being human, and accepting that is part of self-compassion. As we come to accept this in ourselves, we will be less angry when someone else has the same imperfections. We cannot expect uniformity from our spouse any more than we can expect it of ourselves. Novelist Marcel Proust, who was devoted to exploring the multidimensionality of people, said, "The real voyage of discovery consists not in seeking new landscapes, but in having new eyes."

The value of the exercises below is to help you become more comfortable with ambiguity and the multidimensionality of truth. If you can change the way you look at things and the ground rules you have created in your mind, you will change your susceptibility to anger.

- *A Proustian exercise:* Make a list of the last five things your spouse did that made you angry and give two interpretations of each, other than your original one. One of the interpretations may be from your spouse's point of view. As you do this, ask yourself: Can I be sure my view is 100 percent correct, or could I be 10 percent incorrect? For example, a father brought the children home an hour and a half late from visitation. The mother was furious because she thought she was "disrespected" and that he wanted to show her he could flaunt court orders. Other interpretations could be: (1) he found it difficult to separate from the children; or (2) the children caused delay so they could spend more time with him. If you believe your reasoning process is absolutely correct, then your anger will be stimulated every time you perceive you are violated. This exercise disarms that hair trigger.

- *Writing a letter:* Write a letter to the person you are angry at that you never intend to send. Be as irate as you wish, but try to express the secondary emotions (fear, insecurity, abandonment) behind your anger in the letter. After you are done, destroy the letter. Dumping your emotions on paper affords your brain the opportunity to access different neurological pathways, enabling you to consider your anger more objectively. Writing gives you the feeling of having done something with your anger other than reacting against the person who caused it.

- *Sharing with a third party:* Vent your anger to a close friend, someone who has nothing to do with your situation, who is not involved with your family. One cautionary note: check with the person before you begin to make sure he or she is prepared to listen. If it is not a good time, ask when a better time would be and make plans to talk then. You will also need to be sure the person is a good listener and does not incite you to further anger or negative interpretations. Notice whether your friend has emotional reactions to your situation. If so, the friend is coming from his or her own perspective and experiences and not giving you the objectivity you need. Observe if you feel more agitated or more tired when you are done talking with the friend. If the answer is yes, check in with your own emotional reserves before you decide to have another conversation with that person.

- *Making a "hit list":* Write a list of all the people you are angry at, past and present, and note why. See if any of their offenses have been duplicated by your spouse. Your spouse may be reactivating past offenses in your life that he or she really has nothing to do with.

- *Listening with a different ear:* When others are angry at you, listen until they are finished communicating, and then ask if they are done before you speak. Consider whether there is anything justified in what they say. If so, take responsibility only for the part that may be justified. Don't try to calm them down; if they are at the peak of their anger, they won't calm down until they have finished venting or have exhausted themselves. Practice having conversations with people other than your spouse and hear them out no matter what they are saying. If you start this practice when you aren't really invested, it will be much easier when you are.

I have a short attention span, so I do something I call meditative listening. I try to completely focus on what the other person is saying, breathing deeply while I listen, especially if he or she is saying something that agitates me. I strive to not think about what fabulous point I am going to make when the person is done. I focus as much on my breathing as I do on what is being said. Another way of deflecting anger was explained to me by a Jesuit priest who always used to tell me to pray for my enemies. I have learned that in the act of praying or meditating I am able to release some of the anger. This is also something you can do while you are listening.

- *Realizing limited capacities:* Make a list of your spouse's limitations. For example, "He is unable to handle conflict," or, "In her family they don't communicate about feelings, so she never learned how." As you write this list, notice that it would have been difficult for your spouse to act any way other than how he or she did. The behavior may not have been as intentional as you suppose. Perhaps family history, emotional experiences, or someone else's influence (including an attorney's) induced the behavior. Another's offensive behavior may have been the best that he or she could do. It is hard to be angry at the sky for having clouds.
- *Walking:* If you are angry, go for a walk. Walking is a highly effective technique for reducing anger. In my courtroom during negotiations or even during a trial, I may tell the litigants and the lawyers to take a walk for ten minutes. Anger causes the adrenals to start pumping adrenaline. Research has indicated that a walk can produce chemicals that act as pain relievers and promote relaxation. Walking releases endorphins, which are feel-good chemicals. Ac-

cording to Dr. John Ratey, walking releases tryptophan into the bloodstream, which is a necessary ingredient for mood stabilization.[4] When you get angry, you tense your muscles. When you walk, your heart increases blood flow throughout your body, which warms your muscles. Your joints produce a lubricating fluid that releases the tension in your body. Walking increases oxygen in the brain, particularly if you walk outside, and a well-oxygenated brain helps you get clarity. Of course, exercise has the same beneficial effect, but sometimes we are too angry to exercise, so just start walking.

- *Meditation:* Thousands of books have been written about the value of meditation. It decreases confusion, enhances clarity, instills calm, orders chaotic thinking, and clears the mind. If you do it, it will deliver.

- *Realizing that anger fades:* Make a list of five things in your life that you were very, very angry about that no longer mean as much (or anything) to you. As you make this list, you will realize that what is angering you now is just another one of the things that will shortly lose its intensity.

When you heat metal with fire, the molecular consistency of the metal becomes stronger. Similarly, each time you come back from conflict in a positive way, your postmarriage relationship becomes more resilient. To allow for disagreement is to allow the other person to be him- or herself, not just some idealized version of a spouse required by your fantasy. That real person will at times let you down. In fact, everyone will disappoint you at one time or another. The people closest to you will behave badly from time to time (if you don't think so, just be honest about your own behavior and about those whom you have let down). You must allow your spouse the same slack and understanding that you will need from time to time.

Anger-management classes teach that repressing anger is not effective. Enhancing compassion is far more successful in the process of decreasing anger. To be compassionate is to be understanding and gentle with another person who is struggling. If you used to have compassion for the person you once loved, it is easier to have it now. If you did not understand your spouse's point of view during the marriage, it is more difficult, though hardly impossible, to access it now. In the next chapter we will roll up our sleeves and look at behavior where compassion is given in a very low dosage, if at all. Betrayal.

5

Carnival Mirrors

Betrayal

When we find out our spouse is having an affair, we invariably believe that: *Betrayal is a crime against the soul; it has a persistent quality that maims the spirit. Although other injuries may heal, this one cannot, as it has burrowed like an alien into our heart. There is no reparation to our memories, and this kind of scar can never be resurfaced. Our psyche had sustained damage beyond compensation.*

From the moment you learn your spouse has been unfaithful, you lacerate yourself with questions: "Shouldn't I have known?" "This is my life partner—did I allow the betrayal through some failure or mistake?" "Does this new love somehow know or understand my spouse better than I do?" "Shouldn't I have known from the beginning that my beloved was capable of deception?" As you spiral down through the pain, you backtrack through every incident that told your gut something was amiss. Then you blame yourself for ignoring your instincts.

In your heart you believed that the relationship had finally ripened to the point where you didn't have to be on guard. With trust you thought you could relax; you did, and it was delicious. And now it feels as if your life has been stolen from you when you were asleep. You could have defended yourself, had you only known. Now you know the truth. Betrayal is a secret battlefield you are unaware of until you are defeated.

Becoming Sherlock Holmes

Trying to figure out what is and is not true as a result of your spouse's affair is like using carnival mirrors to get an accurate picture of yourself. You can no longer be sure when you were loved and when you were not, when your spouse was or wasn't where he or she was supposed to be, or what the tipping point was that left your spouse vulnerable to temptation. The past cannot be calculated or measured; you don't know when you were loved 95 percent of the time or when it dropped to 60 percent.

To survive, we attempt to reconstruct an ordered and accurate pattern of facts about what really happened. Reeling and still in disbelief, we try to piece together a new reality. We want to establish a reality that is so accurate we can almost see it with our eyes—then we can create our "theory of the crime." In so doing, we embark on a circular and painful endeavor, as this information cannot be captured in time or space. It is as if, while walking in the dark in a familiar place—a place we know as well as the back of our hand—we stumble and fall down a staircase we didn't even know was there. We try to make sense of every dot on this pointillist canvas, hoping to reduce the pain. But the dots are in the millions, and the search takes all the energy we have.

Maybe you can remember the day you fell in love, but it is almost impossible to pinpoint the day you fell out of it. In your desperate and frantic attempt to catalogue emotional history (which defies measurement), you can drive yourself into a state of constant mental agitation. You may find one answer, and in an hour that answer changes. And when your bearings are lost, the thing you cling to should not be a thought process that contains inaccurate facts arranged in a fractured picture. Once you begin re-creating the crime scene, there are unlimited kaleidoscopic realities, leaving you with blurred vision and optical illusions.

As you come to realize the difficulty of re-creating the past, you may crave the truth so strongly that you try to wrest it from your offending spouse. Beware of this blind alley. A spouse will lie or shade the truth for any of several reasons. If she still cares for you, she will try to spare you the pain of the secret courtship. If the betrayal was some sort of retaliation or was anger-based, he may make the story even worse than it really was, in an effort to increase your pain. Why allow more power to be shifted to someone likely to offer answers that can only compound the ambiguity?

I recommend an alternative approach. It is the only one I believe offers a chance to choose the lens through which you will perceive your circumstances. The elemental power accessible in the case of betrayal does not come from how well you emulate Sherlock Holmes, but from your choice of attitude. There is no power to be gained by becoming attached to an inaccurate and incomplete picture of a horrifying reality. Instead, there is a way to reframe the pain so that it transforms your present into a platform for growth.

The demolition of your old reality has caused your optimism to become severely impoverished. But what are you really hungry for? In truth, it is not answers about the specifics of the betrayal. What you really need is a "superfood" that addresses accessing your own power. This "superfood" will allow you to detach from negative thought processes, unhook from your story line about your devastation, and release the other person to his or her own fate.

When you find out about the deception, you fall into truth. The truth is that your mate has unknowable, unpredictable, and mutable parts. In the beginning we all think we know our partner. Betrayal tells us what we already knew deep down: reality is not permanent, and for that reason complete truth is unknowable. Yes, betrayal is the far end of the spectrum of this idea, but it is the perfect vehicle for exemplifying impermanence. You have now been forced to accept that impermanence is part of the life cycle of human existence. Permanency and loyalty are beautiful objectives, but their loss should not be a basis for our self-destruction. That would be like destroying ourselves over the laws of living. You cannot resist those laws any more than you can oppose the laws of gravity. When you resist change, more suffering happens. Spiritual leaders tell us to do our best when choosing our actions and not to be attached to the results. Betrayal proves—albeit in an undesirable way—the importance of that concept.

The devastating knowledge of betrayal winds its way through every square inch of the relationship: trust, security, love, meaning of life, and ego. When you have been betrayed, it is hard to know what to do or how to feel. To cope with this, you might reach for the heavy artillery. In all likelihood, you will summon commando-grade anger to feel more powerful, hoping your anger will devour other, more painful emotions. In this situation, anger is not only abundant, but primitive and righteous. Anger is the liquid that pours from a severed reality. The opportunity for handling anger is now at its highest peak and its most difficult. Then, fortified by concepts that underlie the Good Karma Divorce, you do the unthinkable. You step out of the plane into thin air, and you believe in the parachute.

Your parachute is your ability to reframe the present. Accept the facts, but let the importance of your own process be the overriding factor. Accept that impermanence, randomness, hypocrisy, and betrayal are in the world. We are all vulnerable, but we are not doomed.

I will say the word "forgiveness" now, and I will talk about it much more in subsequent chapters. For now, suspend your disbelief. Forgiveness in this context means letting go, releasing the betrayer to his or her fate. You have not been asked to be the historian, the reconciler, the forensic pathologist, or the judge and jury of your marriage. Believe it or not, the facts don't even matter much, in the end. Your circumstances are not terminal. You are not ill-fated, and this is not too brutal to be borne.

If my advice seems harsh or even inapplicable, please know that there is really no other choice, except endless destructive thoughts engendered by the betrayal. You may have to work the chapter on forgiveness twice as hard. You have been devastated, and recovering requires the ultimate in devotion to the processes in this book. This kind of anger is recurring, slow healing, and clinging. Therefore, this pain, like an alarm clock, will remind you to work on your process; it won't let your practice fall through the cracks, and you will have a daily opportunity to exercise a new way to get out of pain.

In Annie Dillard's book *The Maytrees*, the husband, Toby Maytree, cheats on his wife, Lou, with her best friend, Deary. Deary and Toby then move in together. For many years, Lou suffers as a result of the betrayal. One day, Lou considers a different approach:

For one minute by her watch, she imagined liking Maytree impartially. For only one minute by her watch she saw him for himself. That day, having let go one degree of arc only, for one minute, she sighted relief. Here was something she could do. . . . Within a month she figured that if she ceded that the world did not center on her, there was no injustice or betrayal.[1]

Jealousy and Betrayal: How They Affect Your Case

People often feel betrayed even when they don't want to be in the relationship anymore. Once you have adapted to separation, if your spouse connects with someone new, you must adapt to yet another reality. You have worked so hard to find habitable the reality that your marriage just could not make it. Now you have to find consolation within a still harsher reality. Because of the third party's presence, you question whether your marriage was given a fair chance, even if you were already estranged when the affair began. It is easier to accept that the marriage just did not work than to realize the deck may have been stacked against its survival.

I have witnessed the disastrous results when one spouse gets involved with another person before the other spouse. This is often true whether or not the uncoupled spouse still wants the estranged spouse. When a third party comes along and an attachment begins, it becomes even more difficult for a dialogue to continue between the husband and wife. The unattached person feels unheard, left talking to him- or herself, with a former partner too preoccupied to listen or perhaps too influenced by the new love.

I always discourage spouses from bringing their new love into the courtroom. When they do, the case becomes nearly impossible to settle. I remember a case in which the wife regularly brought her new boyfriend to court, essentially pouring acid into the husband's open wounds. Because she seemed to be intentionally causing him pain, it was difficult for him to agree to her requests. The wife appeared to have a support system in the form of her new boyfriend, and the husband felt he did not have one. This increased his resentment and sense of isolation. Her boyfriend was a psychologist, and when she communicated with her husband, she used a new vocabulary. Every time she used the word "boundaries," it seemed he lowered his offers for settlement. He knew they were not her words, and he was sure he was negotiating not only with his wife, but the "shrink" as well.

If your spouse becomes attached to a third party prior to the completion of the divorce process, in your imagination he or she is off having wonderful sex with a new love (and when they are not having sex, they are laughing together—maybe at you). Perhaps you think your spouse has skipped out on the responsibility for the required amount of suffering time. This is when it becomes seductive to use the courtroom process to erase the perceived smile from your spouse's face. "Let's see if he [or she] can still laugh after an extended and combative divorce," a little voice in your head may be saying.

I know from years in the courtroom that the most common way for the unattached spouse to penetrate a situation in which he or she no longer feels relevant is through verbal warfare—words unleashed (perhaps via an attorney) that raise welts on the skin of the soul. Raw, red, and festering, this torrent of accusation is guaranteed to give the new lovers a bad time. It is exactly these kinds of sentiments that attach more to you than your offending spouse. The emotion here is so readily available that you may find it hard to resist. But the choice is clear: if you don't resist you will have scarred yourself far greater than the original offense. For those already in another relationship you might want to remember: you are already engaged in a court process—perhaps in court all too often—it is not a good idea to commit an offense when you are already so close to the gallows.

Every situation is different, but more often than you can imagine, people who have affairs are on a journey that is theirs alone. They may have emotional business that has not been completed. The battle you were not invited to attend is the inner battle with their demons that you did not know about. The betrayal may have been activated by something other than you, and you were pulled into something of which you may have been ignorant. I offer no excuses for those who stray, but try to propose a method for understanding: Betrayal is not always personal.

Many times the affair has nothing to do with who you are or are not. You may say, "Still, the vows say loyalty and monogamy." The concept of a vow is adherence to a promise. The vows are meant to be sacred, but a vow is really an aspiration. And your spouse's unilateral decision that the vows no longer apply is not a license for you to destroy your life with anger. The betrayal was only the crust of the pie. The life lessons in the marriage are the whole pie, and you will miss them if you focus only on the crust.

My friend Marie had numerous affairs during her eight-year marriage, which ended in 1995. She always spoke of them to me as if she was having the time of her life, until recently, when I asked her if she had any regrets, then or now. She said she hadn't thought about it in a long time and then with full release told me:

> Whatever I did back then, I thought I was totally justified. You make up any story to yourself, to justify what you are doing. I always thought of myself as the kind of person who would never do that; I couldn't even understand people who did. The guilt I feel now is about that moment when I crossed over to the dark side. I just didn't want to take responsibility for my life; I wanted to blame him for what I was going to do to get out of pain. And that is what I wanted, just to get out of pain. I feel guilty because I didn't have to go to the dark side, but I couldn't figure out another way.
>
> Looking back, I expected more of myself. After the first affair it got easier in a way. But after a while, I was just out there. I wasn't really safe at home, because I didn't want to be around my husband; I was afraid he would ask me questions and I would get caught. He became the enemy, so I started to resent him for making me feel guilty. You are now in a no-man's-land. You can't go home—there is no more comfort there, as you have contaminated it with lies—and you are vulnerable "out there." I was getting my fix, but it was eating me up alive. But after a while, you have to lie more, and watch every lie to try and keep it consistent. I then had to start lying to my friends, and the rest of my family. I was even thinking about my lies in my

dreams. After a while you start to believe your lies. The thing is it always follows you; you think it will go away, but it doesn't.

I asked her what it was that really hurt her about being deceptive. She said:

It messes up what you believe about yourself, and no matter how long it takes, it works against you. You unconsciously do things that sabotage your life. It distorts your vision about what good things you should be entitled to. I always wanted the dream; I never saw myself as someone who would end up lying and cheating. Until you get real with yourself and come to terms about why you were the way you were, who you hurt, which is everyone, no holds barred, you continue to do unconscious penance. Your life decisions are distorted.

This is hardly the picture of two blissful people in a love-filled villa in Acapulco. Deceivers must view everyone as dangerous and capable of taking away their family, social status, and credibility. Anyone who finds out can take away their power. As they start telling what they call white lies to everyone, distinctions of right and wrong get blurred. Also, lies travel in packs; each one needs five others to support it. This requires energy and nonstop attention to detail.

After talking to Marie, I realized that deceivers need tools for self-examination that lead to self-forgiveness and the forgiveness of the entire family. Which would you rather be—someone who was deceived but has a firm path and remedies for recovery, or someone without any such tools? If you read books that give you tools for tolerating suffering, you know that even with these tools the path is hard; imagine how hard it is for those with no tools. If they have no methods for self-forgiveness or finding the value of apologies, and no philosophy to set anchor in turbulent waters, they will stay in pain. What if escaping to a third person is all they can do? They may have no idea that there is anything else they can do with their pain.

Betrayers' deception blocks them from attaining peace. This is true, even though it may be invisible. We imagine that they don't suffer, that they are joyous and indulging every desire. And because they seem to do so without payment, we believe they have gotten away with it. But no matter how it looks to you, betrayers are the ones who are lost in confusion, may have guilt forever, and must carry the burden of lies.

If you allow me this anarchistic idea, the real answer to minimizing the effects of betrayal is compassion. I am not saying you should feel bad for deceivers or that their struggle should eclipse your own pain, but there is another way to look at this. Those who spent all that energy on deception, without the opportunity for healing, are those who may be marked for life. I have always thought I would rather be the one who sometimes experienced unkind and destructive treatment than be one who was unkind and destructive. To be on the receiving end is just a passing experience, but those who harbor those destructive tendencies must live with or resist those urges each day. Their misdeeds are the basis for our compassion. It is our compassion that will disengage us from this brutal cycle.

Dave married Jennifer, a much younger woman. When their marriage dissolved, Dave remained consumed with guilt and the searing pain of failure until he found out Jennifer had been having an affair with her ex-boyfriend. During the divorce process, Jennifer had dental work performed by Dave's dentist. Soon thereafter, Jennifer and the dentist began a relationship. When Dave learned that Jennifer was sleeping with his dentist, his anger subsided. He began to believe that she could not be monogamous and that perhaps her hunger for validation by men might never be satiated. Ultimately, it took a dentist to show Dave that Jennifer's infidelity wasn't personal. Only when he began to let go of the idea that he was the one who was flawed were they able to begin working toward settling the case. He had realized that his struggles would soon be over, but hers might not be.

As the judge of your own inner courtroom, weigh the karmic evidence. Does your spouse's crime determine *your* sentence? Throughout history, betrayal has been enough to bring down empires. It is the one action done by another that has been viewed as insurmountable. My courtroom offers me a front-row seat at the unfolding of this most tragic of human events. As hard as it is to believe, I can tell you that even the intensity of this pain can be reduced. The longer you wait to attempt to reduce it, however, the more you risk defining yourself by that betrayal. You don't want to add yourself to the list of tragic historical figures.

It is not necessary that you forgive or ever even understand why betrayal happened. It is only necessary that you save yourself by un-hooking. If you can do this when you have been betrayed, the rest of the book's lessons should come more easily, as should the rest of your life. In the next chapter, you will find that there is nothing that you will be experiencing during your divorce that you cannot use to your benefit.

6

Mood Lighting

Emotions as a Source of Illumination

Life is a rainbow which also includes black.
—YEVGENY YEVTUSHENKO

Some organize the process of divorce into stages to endure. I believe the bombardment of emotions happens simultaneously and furiously, like a Cuisinart with the lid off. The needs of the heart, brain, and soul get tangled as they all run for cover from pain simultaneously.

Most of us would do anything to avoid negative feelings, but during a divorce positive feelings seem almost nonexistent. A divorce can throw us off balance and leave us in extremely moody states, well beyond the expected anger and sadness. We may feel embarrassment at our profound rage, humiliation at our exposed "failure," fear of being alone, and guilt and regret over the uncontrollable emotions we have exposed others to, especially our children.

The art comes in knowing how to turn difficult feelings into opportunities for growth instead of letting those emotions fertilize an embittered life. Every emotion you have has a unique way of illuminating a different aspect of your life. "Mood lighting" is a phrase I use to refer to the illumination we can derive from our moods or emotions. Mood lighting identifies some of the most difficult emotions and states of mind to determine how their harmful effects can be minimized and, above all, what benefits can be derived from them. By understanding their benefits, we can resist judging our lives as being either pleasurable or painful, but know that these emotions are part of our personal evolutionary process. Our emotions are not in lockstep with each other; we can make progress with some of them while others heal at a different speed. The same mother who greatly improved her handling of turning the children over for visitation to her husband threw his toolbox in the river the next day. As we notice our own inconsistency, it should be no surprise that our spouse is inconsistent as well.

Like many threadbare proverbs, "Time heals all wounds" is overworked to our disadvantage. It is true that the mind will, in self-defense, create a protective coating against pain, so the pain will dissipate and compensatory emotions will develop. But we can do better than that. If we just leave things alone, they may change, but not in a way over which we have any influence. Our compensations will be random, and we may change in a twisted way by accumulating too much of one emotion and not enough of another. For example, we may compensate for self-pity by staying angry.

Self-awareness often creates a conscious goal to change. Conscious change knows that in the ecology of our emotions everything has to go somewhere, that there is no real throwing away, and that in the landfill of our emotional dump, it would be best to process our waste material and have a hand in determining what it becomes.

In your Personal Manifesto you formulated a path; this chapter will light that path. When you start to realize the benefits of each difficult emotion, you will know you are not suffering for nothing. These emotions are necessary to your metamorphosis, and unless you have felt their impact, you can't own it and your growth is just intellectual. As you stand back and observe these emotions, you are watching them rather than being blindly led by them. Watching yourself move through these mental states—the essence of self-awareness—is a way to use the emotions in a beneficial way. You go from being the raw material of a mental state to the sculptor of it.

Our future remains a mystery. When difficulty strikes, we cannot know how long it will remain or when happiness will return. Regardless of our spiritual orientation, all religions tell us that life is always changing. Difficulty turns into pleasure, pleasure sometimes turns into pain, and so on. Emotions have no solid form; by definition they are fluid. While we are waiting for the winds of change to take us to a more tolerable emotional state, maybe we can sift the sands for the treasures to be found.

With exquisite precision our seemingly unique pain is speaking to us. This pain is knocking on our door, asking us to search for and discover what we really need to change in our life. When we refuse to attend to the knocking, that pain will only knock louder. Most of my life lessons have required a falling meteor to hit me on the head to get my attention. One way or another, pain will get your attention. You want to recognize the different faces of your discomfort, so you know what to do about each one. Each one must be handled differently. If you know how to handle the pain, it cannot have total authority over you.

When I went through my last divorce, I took an inventory of my feelings: I felt invigorated that I would soon be done with a difficult situation, mortified that I was going to get divorced again, sad at the loss of the life we had built together, irritated that I was going to have to take out my "leather miniskirt" and date again, and fearful that I would be carving the turkey alone on Thanksgiving and probably would fall on the knife. All of this was choreographed to the old anthem of self-pity: "How could this happen to me if I am so wonderful?" This was the anthem I sang as I sailed into my Bermuda Triangle. In this black hole I was sure I would dissolve without a partner.

Overwhelmed with confusion, I made a chart of all the emotions I felt, so that when one appeared, I wasn't ambushed: sadness, loneliness, self-pity, depression, fear, anger, resentment, and lack of self-esteem. I began to recognize that anxiety may be fear of the future and not ill health. I started to distinguish when I was feeling guilty from when I didn't like myself. During that time, I felt humiliated at a party, because I forgot my high-heeled shoes and showed up in gym shoes, while everyone else was looking perfect and tall (and coupled). I went home and pulled out my list. I realized that it was not my outfit that was draining my self-esteem, but a bout of fear about the future. Will I always be alone, and in gym shoes? Although I don't welcome that fear, I recognize and identify it, and I know from experience that it will pass. Thus, when fear, anxiety, or sadness appears, I think I know what is happening, so I am not incapacitated by an unknown feeling.

The Fear of Not Knowing

Perhaps the most frightening consequence of divorce is the uncertainty of it all; one of the reasons many unhappy couples stay married is the comfort of predictability. In a marriage or relationship, we experience a lifestyle that repeats day after day and lulls us into believing we know our future. One of the great attributes of married life is the busyness of interaction, which distracts us from the reality that life is unpredictable. You wake up, and there is the animal comfort of someone warm next to you. You know there is someone to call you during the day, even for just a fragrance of conversation. The dreaded fear of Saturday night alone has melted into a thing of the past. But now we realize that any certainty about what we thought our life was supposed to be was only an illusion. We devote much mental attention to trying to make true what is not true—that our life will be predictable. Marriage serves a useful purpose of numbing the anxiety about the truth that we can never know tomorrow. When you become separated from your mate, the comfort about the predictability of life is removed.

When we start to accept that we cannot know the future, we are unavoidably in a receptive state. In this state we seek new ways to view our life. Now we have the opportunity to create a new picture beyond what we could have ever envisioned. The opposite of fear of the unfamiliar is curiosity about it.

Transformational Warm-up

Would you consider being curious about your new life rather than letting your thoughts be dominated by fear? When we are curious and therefore more open, there is no need to evaluate events as positive or negative—we just meet reality as it unfolds. Curiosity always exists within us, but it will become eclipsed by fear when apprehensions about our future are amplified. Fear plays as loud heavy metal, while curiosity plays as soft lyrical jazz. Irish novelist James Stephens wrote, "Curiosity will conquer fear even more than bravery will." Curiosity not only eases our fear of the unknown, but can be a great ally on our path of self-awareness about the significance of our difficulty.

Curiosity can stimulate truthful inquiry about our marriage. Questions will arise: "Why did the relationship fall apart?" "Why did my spouse leave?" "I knew we had some troubles, but not to the point of divorce! What happened?" If we can allow curiosity to guide us instead of lament and fear, we can identify issues that need our attention. Inspirational author William Arthur Ward tells us, "Curiosity is the wick in the candle of learning." Before the wick burns out, try to grasp the lessons to be learned. And the candle burns brightest when we are in pain.

Although we strive to get comfortable with the idea of not knowing our future, that does not mean we shouldn't cultivate intentions about how we would like our future to be. The other powerful weapon against the fear of not knowing our future is the horsepower of intention. In the creation of your manifesto and devotion to the intentions outlined in it, you will find powerful tools to minimize the fear of not knowing. You have created your intentions about who you desire to be. This is important. You are not leaving it up to chance or designing your future in reaction to someone else's behavior or decisions.

Take a look at some of the unexpected outcomes in your life:

• Make a list of difficult situations you have been in where the outcome was unexpected and ultimately rewarding.

Here are two of mine. If I hadn't needed knee surgery, I never would have been able to sit still long enough as I recovered to begin this book. If I'd had money when I desperately needed it to help support our child, I would have never been ambitious enough to go to law school.

Self-Pity: Self-Destruction Without the Explosives

Despair is the absolute extreme of self-love. It is reached when
a man deliberately turns his back on all help from anyone else in
order to taste the rotten luxury of knowing himself to be lost.
—Thomas Merton

Self-pity is a much-criticized emotion. There is a difference between self-pity and compassion directed toward oneself. It is necessary
to be gentle and patient with oneself to promote the healing process. I
don't completely agree that an interlude of self-pity should be harshly
judged. It is a state of mind that helps us transition between a painful
reality and compassion for ourselves. Provided it is not done for an extended period of time, I think it has value.

Wallowing in self-pity is an attempt to get used to a new sadness in
our heart and body. It is a place to rally from, not a mind state to skip. It
is also the emotion we fall into when we are fatigued. Because self-pity
has an adhesive quality, it takes effort to keep this way of coping with
sorrow from turning into a permanent approach to life.

Because self-pity is at the bottom of the list of acceptable emotions, we often criticize ourselves for engaging in it. When we do, the
effect is very punishing, because we are duplicating what was already
done to us, yet again. To criticize ourselves for feeling bad about our
predicament only serves to make us feel worse about feeling bad. A
friend might say, "You shouldn't feel so bad about your divorce; after
all, Mary's child is in the hospital and people are drowning in Ban-
gladesh." But those statements don't make us immediately feel better
about our situation. As a matter of fact, sometimes we feel worse that
the plight of a child or the Bangladeshis doesn't make us grateful for
what we do have that you might want.

Another seducer that inspires self-pity is comparing yourself to
other married couples. Such comparisons may be false and based on
inaccurate perceptions. You have no idea of the full circumstances of
the couple to whom you are comparing yourself. It is your illusion that
they have something you want, and your illusion may not be factual
about what they have that you might want. The heart of self-pity is the

conviction that the rewards of life are unjustly distributed. It is your current sadness that muddies your vision as you do your calculations about who is blessed and who is cursed. Do you really know their history and what sadness they have known?

Once you feel sorry for yourself, all your positive attributes are disregarded. For example, you cannot feel sorry for yourself and at the same time take pleasure in the fact that you are an excellent musician. You might intellectually believe you are an excellent musician, but self-pity tells you that really doesn't matter. The danger of self-pity is that it stations a Rottweiler at the gate of positive emotions.

However, when you are lamenting about what you do not have or what you have lost, you often find out what it is you truly want. For example, Christmas with family might now be more important to you than ever before. If your spouse's side of the family no longer talks to you, you might know for the first time how much family contact means to you. You feel abandoned. Now you know what to do. You need to cultivate more relationships. Used effectively, self-pity is a springboard, a call to action.

Tools for Dealing with Self-Pity

During those times when a friend of mine was going through some devastating heartbreak, I found that if we could create a *plan of action*, she would suddenly become energized. For her, we broke the cycle of being stuck in self-pity.

- Make a plan of action that targets exactly what you are feeling badly about. The plan does not have to be extraordinary. It does not have to be permanent. It doesn't even have to be smart. I suggest getting a friend to help you create a plan of action. It is the motion away from this emotion that counts. It just has to rock the boat.

Here's an example of what a plan might look like. My friend was worried about her finances, and she had given up speaking with friends connected with the relationship that had ended. She was a furniture designer and had not paid attention to her work for years. We decided she was going to send out announcements about a new location for her business (even though it was her apartment), call three people a week who had been clients, and resume her work.

The obvious and most powerful weapon against self-pity is feeling *gratitude*. If you think that is easy, think again. Your marriage or relationship has just fallen apart, but, as mentioned, trying to make yourself feel gratitude by comparing yourself with those less fortunate doesn't often work. The easiest way to access gratitude is to be grateful for the small accomplishments along *your* transforming path.

- Make a list of the things you are grateful for. Try to include as many items as possible, both large and small. Be sure to include intangibles like experiences, insights, and newfound knowledge. (This is also valuable for journaling or reflection at the end of the day.)

For example, when you were married you spent most of your time with your spouse. Now you have two new friends you never would have had time for before. Gratitude. Your youngest daughter always needed special attention, but with the turmoil in your marriage you couldn't summon the extra energy she needed. You give it to her now almost every day. Gratitude. Your neighbor divorced a few years ago. She was always sad, and that irritated you. You now understand the situation and want to help her. You now have the tools to help her. Gratitude.

When self-pity is allowed to linger, it weakens the psyche, allowing all of the other negative emotions to bombard you. This is where you risk depression. But even depression delivers its own formula with healing properties.

The Gifts of Depression Can Be the Most Profound

My last fond memory of depression occurred when my relationship with my second husband went from "tying the knot" to a knot in my heart. That knot was created by the realization that my marriage was going to end in divorce. Yes, I feared the unknown, but more than that, I feared slowly slipping into the sticky tar of all moods: depression. I believe depression happens when we fall to our knees, because we can no longer bear the weight of battling our other difficult emotions. Our emotional batteries have run down. Oh yes, we thought we could deal with a little sadness here, a little anxiety there. We put one in our pocket for later and the other in a bottom drawer, hoping to forget about them. Then our life crisis comes, the breakdown of our relationship, and we no longer have the resources to keep the battle going, to keep our emotions tucked away. Though these emotions have been demanding to be heard, we don't want to hear them.

The strength to fight this depression is hard to access. Depression is the kitchen sink ("sink" being both literal and figurative here) of all emotions, because you have to fight not to slip down the drain. Depression makes you feel as though you're not fighting the good fight and you fear paralysis setting in. Your world starts to get smaller, and you feel your options becoming fewer and fewer. Simultaneously, when they are needed most, you don't even let your allies and friends move in to help you. You can't find me when I am depressed. I am embarrassed, and I suspect other people feel it is contagious.

Here is where the gifts of depression are probably the most profound. Depression is the Dirty Harry of emotions, and you are staring down the barrel of a gun. Shift or perish. The gift is that you realize you could not have made changes in your life unless you'd hit bedrock, where all the adjustments in your life are waiting to be unearthed. As diarist Anaïs Nin wrote, "And the day came when the risk it took to remain tight inside the bud was more painful than the risk it took to blossom."

His Holiness the Dalai Lama says in his notes about depression that "being self-absorbed has an immediate effect of narrowing one's focus and blurring one's vision. It is like being pressed down by a heavy load." The "pressing down" (which I believe is the heart of depression) is that we are pressed into surrender. Depression has put our emotions under anesthesia to spare us pain. Although anesthesia has its place for numbing pain during surgery, too much of it for too long a time is not healthy.

Yoga master B.K.S. Iyengar says, "When everything else is stripped away, the essential is revealed." Depression strips other emotions of their intensity, so you are now able to come to grips with more than just getting out of pain—you can deal with the profound issues of your existence. When everything is going smoothly, why would you be motivated to ask the essential questions about your life? In addition, depression forces you to deal with things that may be at the bottom of your grief, fear, and sadness. There alone is where all of the real issues ferment. If you are booked on a trip to Death Valley against your will, get your pan out and start sifting for gold.

This discussion deals mainly with aspects of situational depression, not clinical depression. The approach presented here should not be considered a replacement for professional treatment for a serious psychological condition or the possible need for medication. However, the discussion and suggestions may help ease depression and minimize its recurrence.

Suggestions for Dealing with Depression

Because of depression's immobilizing effect, what you need are *panoramic perspectives* and *to-do lists*. They are more important now than usual.

- Leave the house and go somewhere you can watch other people participating in their lives. There's something very releasing in the feeling you are part of the rest of the world and not isolated in misery that has been chosen just for you.
- Make a list of what you want to accomplish that day. Your self-starter is stalled, so a detailed list really helps. The list may include such simple items as "Have lunch," "Call Jim," or "Walk for fifteen minutes." This to-do list firms up a plan and is the opposite of starting your day by reacting to random negative emotions.

Remember the last time you went through trauma, how you struggled to find a silver lining, and in the end you did? By observing how your *suffering* turned out to be *beneficial*, you can see the unique way it served you.

- Make a list of ways you have suffered in your life. Then next to each entry, write down how you have changed as a result of that suffering.

If there are times of suffering that you cannot yet squeeze benefits out of, hold on to this list, highlight that part with a yellow marker, and revisit it later on in the journey. Often it is difficult to see how the suffering can benefit you until later.

Another useful tool at this time is *writing*. Novelist Don DeLillo says: "Writing is a concentrated form of thinking. Writing has the power to define things, and define muddled experience."

- Sit down and write about anything that is on your mind. Talk to the page. For example, write about your day in court, your anger and resentments, what your ideal life would look like, what qualities your new mate might have, what you would ideally like to tell the judge if you get a chance, what items you need to review with your lawyer, or what difficult circumstances and conversations you need to have with your children.

Your writing does not have to be edited; it does not have to be literary or even good. The interesting thing about writing is that you don't have to work on finding a new way of seeing things; when you write, new perceptions will appear. Guaranteed.

These suggestions will help you fight the paralyzing effects of depression and facilitate self-excavation from the pit. One of the biggest potential obstacles to overcoming depression is fear of our newly found time alone.

The Atmosphere of Alone

When we are coupled, companionship fills up the room. But now we dread the long seemingly empty days and endless nights. These lonely hours can be our greatest allies, and yet we call them the enemy. They're only the enemy if we fear them; they are our friend if we find a way to profit from them. In a perfect world we would work one day, experiencing all the stress that goes with it, and rejuvenate the next. The piercingly lonely time can be turned into rejuvenation for the next day.

Being alone is a good time to call yourself to account, to see what you have mastered that day, or to see what you yet want to accomplish or do better. The evening alone is also the time to unload your burdens of the day. In the evening there is not much more to do about the day's problems and torments other than get yourself reloaded for the next day. What do you do to reload? Maybe you have not put aside much time that is solely dedicated to rejuvenating your spirit and body. The re-loading time is as essential as firing time. We live in a culture where we are encouraged to always be productive. Ours is one of the few cultures that does not revere rest as the foundation from which productivity and creativity are launched.

Our minds trick us into believing we must attain continual happi-ness or continually feel good. When that becomes the goal, then we have judged our loneliness as either good or bad, not just a state of being. Aloneness and even loneliness is not the enemy; it can be used as part of the natural process of life. When we have filled our life with people just for the sake of filling it, then, according to the laws of physics, there is no space for something new to come into it. I have heard it said that the path to wisdom may be confusion. The atmosphere in which confusion might forge wisdom may very well be temporary loneliness.

Transformational Warm-ups

Loneliness is not only missing your spouse, but yearning for the smell of Sunday morning breakfast or opening presents on Christmas Eve. What are some of the *things you miss*, things you loved that are no longer in your life?

- Make a list of the things you are currently missing in your life and note what it is about each that you find desirable. If possible, prioritize them. The more you miss certain things, the more you know you want to duplicate them in your life now and in your next relationship.

Working for the welfare of others takes our mind off its incorrect belief in its own isolation. Ask any recovering alcoholic, and you will find out that the best way to counteract loneliness is to volunteer and help others.

- Volunteer in some capacity, offer to help someone, or simply do something that you see needs doing. You don't have to rush out to a soup kitchen on a Saturday night. Just call a friend who could really use some conversation. Thank them for something they contributed to your life.

One antidote to loneliness is filling up your time with friends and outside activities. But that does not address the dread you feel when your door closes and there is no one there but you. *Special activities at home* will reduce the dread of your emotions flooding over you when you are alone. I have often turned my home into an ashram. I may start off the day journaling, cooking interesting food from a new recipe, or listening to new music and lecture tapes on literature and physics.

- Make a list of activities you like to do when you are alone. Include some things you have done in the past as well as some that you have never tried, but would like to.
- When you are at a loss, *do* one of the items on the list.

Fear of Losing Identity

From birth on we are in a process of self-identification. When we are born we are identified by gender and then given a name. We grow up in a family that may be identified by religion or ethnicity; in it we are a brother or sister, daughter or son. Eventually we become a student or professional, husband or wife, mother or father, and so forth. Soon we believe these labels are who we are. As we become so layered over with these identities, the voice from the soul—who we are inside—becomes muffled. As Eckhart Tolle puts it "when you fully accept that you don't know you actually enter a state of peace and clarity that is closer to who you really are than thought could ever be."[2]

A divorce often alters the roles you've been used to. But if you are stripped of a superficial identity, you have the opportunity to build a new identity, one deeper than wife, father, breadwinner, or caretaker. You can now begin to rely on the internal essence of who you are, the you that you know to be there. This is where your identity really lies. Your identity is not angry husband, cheated wife, or alienated parent. Those identities are transitory. Now there is an open space where illusory identity used to be. The great Italian artist Michelangelo said it best: "I did not sculpt the David. I removed the stone that wasn't him."

At first the lack of definition feels too vast and uncertain, because there are no limiting margins. Having margins feels safer, because they give you something to bounce against or something to resist. But if you are open to what you can become and go beyond the limitations of your previous identity, all things are possible. In the beginning of your divorce the vision of your possibilities could have never been large enough, as you scrambled to hold on to old definitions. It is difficult to know your real inside picture when you are focusing only on the frame.

I want to make a point about identity and materialism. I would never advise you to give up what you are entitled to in your divorce negotiations. But too often during a divorce, pursuit of money and assets takes on enhanced importance as things become a reflection of our desired self. We become sure that physical comfort will insulate us from our insecurities. We taint all financial negotiations with this deeper internal quest for security. We are trying to create a more predictable life by getting the dining-room set, and we believe our digestion will be better with lovely furniture. In an attempt to solve our insecurities with material things, another source of suffering is created. Winning a dispute over a material item becomes interpreted as gaining power. This is fundamentally a weakening notion, because you have attached your power to something external. When money and things are confused with identity and power, court battles can always seem justified.

Transformational Warm-up: *Neti, Neti* Exercise

In India there is a spiritual practice called *neti, neti,* meaning "not this, not this," which helps identify that part of us that is our soul.

- Make a list of all your identities: teacher, father, sister, carpenter, dancer, and so on. After each one, ask yourself, "Is this my soul?" and answer "Yes" or "Not this." For example, "I am a real estate developer; *not this.*" "I am a brother; *not this.*"

More often than not, your answer will be "Not this." As you whittle away illusions of what you are, you begin to see how not to confuse identities with your soul. When roles are lost, as they are during divorce, this exercise will allow you to deemphasize the importance of stated roles and emphasize the value of who you are on a deeper level. It is a way of letting go of your insecurities about losing your superficial identities, so they do not block your real identity. The ultimate goal is to separate illusion from reality.

After-Midnight Magic: Insomnia

I told my son, Jonas, I was working on a chapter about the usefulness of even the most negative emotions. Proposing a challenge, he asked me what was good about waking up at three in the morning, because he had so much on his mind. I told him, "Your mind is on a superhighway and is tangled in a gridlock, and you are waking up to unlock it."

Sometimes it is the glare of daylight that obscures what is really bothering you. Problems that nagged at you but seemed benign mid-morning are now menacing you at three o'clock in the morning. In the middle of the night we are forced to concentrate on those problems and convert the nagging angst into a search for solutions. Undistracted.

Sometimes when you can't sleep, it is because there are absolute truths or answers bursting through your dreams begging to be found. I learned to untangle the mental traffic from Julia Cameron, author of *The Artist's Way*. When I wake, unable to sleep, I get out of bed and write down every thought—however ordinary or fantastic, irrelevant or significant, trivial or monumental—that is on my mind. I have to get all the thoughts on the page, so I can start moving the problems into their separate lanes. I can do it best without any distractions, without anyone else in my life being awake, with no one to call, nowhere to go, and nothing on TV except commercials with Ron Popeil gazing lovingly at meat rotating on a hook. In the stillness of the night, my truth and my answers are as close to the surface and authentic as they will ever be. That is my after-midnight magic. I don't look for it, but if it comes looking for me, I am ready. And like James Bond, my pen is going to save my life.

Here are some suggestions to deter insomnia:

1. Don't listen to the news before you go to bed.

2. Don't talk to anyone about anything disturbing after 9 p.m., especially about your case. Unless they can resolve your problem at a late hour, it will just lie on your brain like peanut butter. If possible, deal with difficulties in the morning, when you have all day to work through them.

3. If you watch TV before bed, use the automatic sleep timer, so you don't wake up in the middle of the night because the TV is on.

4. Make sure that your bedroom is organized, peaceful, and aesthetically appealing, so that when you wake up, the first thing you see are pleasant surroundings. In other words, when your defenses are down internally, don't compound this state with chaotic externals.

Distraction: Taking a Break from Pain

The current scientific belief is that everything about the universe ultimately has to do with energy.[3] Our thoughts are electrical impulses, and our emotions are, at their core, energy. The universe, then, is a field of pure potential that is continually moving. Here's the rule: every feeling fully felt creates shifts. In order for there to be healing, there must be feeling. Moving the energy by feeling the emotion rather than by repressing it creates energy centers that are clear and free-flowing. Even tears mean your sadness has good mobility, and your pain has not frozen in your body. Tears are simply liquid pain finding release by escaping from the body. But there is a difference between the harm caused by repressing pain and finding ways to lessen its impact. Distraction is really taking a break from pain.

Arsenic is deadly, but it can be medicinal in small doses. Although I would never want anyone to go through a sustained difficult time, experiencing a short period of challenges, believe it or not, is like a small dose of arsenic—it can be quite medicinal. The danger in negative emotions is not the emotions themselves, but the risk of repetition and rumination. Study after study shows that what you think about is what you give strength and power to. Repetitious thoughts will, in a short time, create patterns that predispose you to repeat those thoughts and actions. It is best to interrupt this cycle as soon as possible.

Keeping a list of potential distractions and interruptions will assist you with the alarmingly regular appearance of negative occurrences during a divorce. The distractions serve to loosen the grip of those cyclical thoughts. Distractions, if absorbing and interesting, work well to divert your attention from the storms of anger, uncertainty, fear, and sadness. Even the mundane, if you can look at it in the context of your transition, is always on the threshold of mystery. Novelist Aldous Huxley tells us, "Happiness is not achieved by the conscious pursuit of happiness; it is generally the by-product of other activities."

My sure-fire distraction has always been a bookstore with a good music department. There is equipment there that allows you to hear thirty seconds of any song on a CD. Whether or not in the end I walk away with new CDs, my main goal will have been accomplished—I will have been distracted, even if only for an hour. I have interrupted the pattern. Once you know that you have an ally in distraction, you begin to know that there is no difficult emotion that cannot be diffused. This is the fundamental lesson in the fluidity of emotion. Even during an emotional tsunami, I have sometimes gone from beyond sadness to Beyoncé in under an hour.

Try to identify a personal rescue pattern that works for you, even if you have never identified it as such. With use, this rescue pattern develops in the Darwinian sense: it helps our species, saturated in breakups, survive. The one thing you have to do is to find a way to shake it up and get out of your routine. It is not important what you do—just make your brain think a different way about something else even for a half hour. Here are some ideas.

• Make a list of enjoyable things you do or have done alone.

The list could include such activities as going to a driving range to practice your golf swing, roaming through a Home Depot or a botanical garden, taking a long walk with a reward at the end like a book or popcorn, rearranging furniture, or making a scrapbook of your children's pictures. The common factor here is that none of these activities depend on the participation of another person. Make this list while you are feeling reasonably good, because if you are in a difficult state of mind, it will be hard to remember what you enjoy.

Next, include others:

• Make a list of activities you like to do with others.

You might think of creating a book club or a practice circle for people going through divorce, scheduling tennis games, finding a walking or workout partner, signing up for a class, or creating an event with your children such as pitching a tent and sleeping in the living room, telling stories and roasting marshmallows.

Finally, people often provide the best distractions:

• Make a list of all of the people in your life, from the inner circle of those closest to you to outer circle, your acquaintances. Next to each person's name, write what special value they have in your life.

A sample list might look like:

Lonnie—great empathizer and funny

Margot—inventive with new ideas

Marty—makes me laugh every time

Fay—gets to the bottom of a problem and puts it into context

Keith—no nonsense and yet sympathetic

Susan—the place to go if you want the wise truth

Melody—the place to go if you want a different version of the truth

A list like this helps you know who to go to for what you need. It will not help you when you are feeling fragile to go to the truth teller, any more than when you are feeling angry to get help from someone to invent something.

Armed with dozens of new strategies and tactics for managing your moods and harnessing the power of even your negative emotional energy, you are now ready to take on the toughest, but perhaps the most valuable aspect of the Good Karma Divorce. You may be sure that your spouse is responsible for all of your struggles, but in Chapter 7 get ready to access power from a surprising source: forgiveness.

7

Forgiveness

Weapon of Mass Construction

Holding on to anger is like grasping a hot coal with the intent of throwing it at someone else; you are the one who gets burned.
—BUDDHA

*H*aven't I done everything possible to try to save this marriage? Isn't he the one who didn't try hard enough? Isn't she the one who started being nasty, when all I wanted to do was be reasonable? *Sure I'm not perfect, but I was only reacting to his behavior!*

Forgiveness is difficult enough with friends or acquaintances, but it is extraordinarily so with a spouse during a divorce. You may have a Rolodex of examples of how your spouse caused you pain, and the odds are you believe it is your mate who is at fault and bears most of the responsibility for what you and your family are enduring.

Forgiveness is easier when you believe someone has a good agenda for you, but when you are going through a divorce, you doubt that your spouse really does. As a matter of fact, you are in a protective stance. The wagons are circling, so the idea of forgiving an adversary feels too risky. You perceive that you would be letting that person back into your vulnerable space. To do this is completely counterintuitive. All of your instincts advise you not to open yourself up, for fear of being hurt again.

Almost from the moment we know we are going to divorce, we start to shuffle the deck of responsibility. We want the cards indicating we may be at fault at the bottom of the deck and those that blame the other person at the top. Initially we might have considered forgiveness, but as the divorce process unfolds, we descend down the ladder, and forgiveness seems farther and farther away. Here are a few rungs on the ladder:

- Your partner tells very intimate details of your marriage to his lawyer.
- You find out your spouse has reported to her friends why she can no longer stand your self-centeredness.
- You are filling out your financial affidavit and must go through the excruciating pain of seeing what your life was and how it will not be the same.
- You are looking at his credit-card statements and wondering why there are so many entries for the Blue Lobster restaurant, a place he always hated. Who is he going there with now?

This is the kind of dialogue I hear:

She: "I never thought he would behave so badly after we separated. I feel like I hardly know him. He used to eat red meat four times a week. Now he's become a vegetarian and lost twenty-five pounds. When we were together, I begged him to eat a healthy diet!"

He: "She's going out with her friends every night—in high heels! When we were together, she never wanted to go out, not even in her gym shoes! And she's getting breast implants—with my money!"

She: "So what if I got implants—he talked about it in court and to everyone he knows. He has become vicious, even though he is the one who left! And you are suggesting I forgive?"

During the divorce process, sympathy and support from your attorney appear indispensable. It seems like a good idea to tell your version tinted in a way that will make you appear more sympathetic. Once your attorney is in the picture, you are often advised to change or terminate your communication with your spouse. When you do communicate with your spouse, it is now manicured so you don't say anything that will jeopardize your legal position. With your conversation now micro-managed, once conflict escalates you no longer use the words that could diffuse hostility by clarifying misperceptions. The anger and distrust just increase, and misconception builds upon misconception.

For example, my friend Brenda was asked by her husband's attorney for her work records. She interpreted that as an attempt by her husband to endanger her job. Had they been communicating, he would have explained to her that his lawyer said it was required by law.

Your lawyer repeats your version over and over in court as well as to the other lawyer. Your belief in your version and the idea that there can be no alternative version become reinforced. In this situation it becomes almost impossible to see what your part in the breakdown of the marriage could be.

When you told your version of the story to your attorney for the first time, you noticed each time you blamed your spouse you got a positive response. When you admitted to some wrongdoing, your lawyer said, "Let's leave that part out." Eventually you do start leaving your part out, even to yourself. You also fear that if you are completely honest with your lawyer, your lawyer might not fight for you as vigorously. This thought process is perilous, because your brain takes in your story as if it were absolute reality; if your story line has you feeling threatened in any way, your brain and body are going to react with fear and release all the chemicals that go with it. With this system of blame and fault, it is too risky to admit to yourself, to your lawyer, to your spouse, and certainly to the court that you had a part in creating the problems. No matter what the law on fault or no-fault is in your state, many people are moored, like a houseboat to a dock, to the concept of "punishing the guilty party."

Forgiveness: The Key to the Puzzle of Human Interaction

Once I gave a speech at a divorce seminar, and when I spoke of forgiveness, a woman raised her hand and said, "I just found out that my husband was seeing prostitutes, not just one—lots of them. I will never forgive him for the rest of my life." She had four children and was vibrating with rage. When I want to see if a new theory of mine works, I always try it out on an extreme example. This was an extreme example. The kind of forgiveness I am talking about in this section is only to help yourself; I reject the belief that the husband's offense would mean she was the one person who was ineligible for the benefits of forgiveness.

Forgiveness as a method for detaching is not the same as reconciliation. Reconciliation is dependent upon interacting with your spouse. Forgiveness is less about the person who harmed you and his or her offenses, no matter how great they may be, than the effect of retained anger on *you*. But in this case, even though she never had to express her forgiveness to her husband, I feared for her, because she seemed to be vowing to stay anchored to her anger forever.

The following categories of behavior are included when I write about using forgiveness to detach from the person who injured you:

- Your spouse intentionally set out to hurt you.
- Your spouse hurt you by disregarding your feelings.
- Your spouse's attorney took actions that hurt you.
- Your spouse's friends or family took actions that hurt you; your spouse either instigated or could have prevented these actions.
- Your spouse hurt the children.
- Your spouse hurt the children to get back at you.
- You believe your spouse did not try hard enough to save the marriage.
- Your spouse did not live up to your ideal of who you wanted him or her to be.
- Your spouse doesn't think he or she did anything wrong and didn't ask for forgiveness.
- Your spouse betrayed you.

Here are some reasons your spouse may have hurt you:

- To cause you to pay for the sins of a prior spouse.
- Because of a romantic involvement with another before the divorce was over.
- Out of his or her own pain or fear.
- Because of a lack of strength to do the right thing or control the actions of their family or an attorney.
- Because of their character, which makes it easy to be oblivious to your pain.
- To retaliate for their own childhood pain.
- As retribution for a perceived injury by you.
- Out of a need to get negative attention when positive attention is no longer forthcoming. It may be very satisfying to provoke you if you are no longer paying attention to them. If they can still hurt you somehow they can still feel significant in your life. Imagine what their mental state must be to go to any lengths to seek attention from you. This person is completely dependent on getting out of pain by causing you pain.
- Because of undue influence by a third party.

Forgiveness Benefits the Forgiver

It is easy to see how complicated it is to analyze people's behavior. You can shake the kaleidoscope a hundred times, each time hoping to find the reasons why someone hurt you, and come up with a different pattern each time. With forgiveness you are releasing yourself from holding on to these questions, the analyzing, the anger and resentment that keeps you Crazy-glued to the one who injured you. Forgiveness is *not* about or for the other party; that person may never know. Forgiveness is for *you*. With forgiveness you can go on with your life unencumbered by ruminative thoughts. You do not have to love the other person again, you are not reconciling, and you do not even have to like him or her again—you only have to like yourself enough to let it go. Forgiveness means you have chosen to let it all go. To let it be. You can now close the door with nothing lingering.

Let's put this concept to a real test. We feel hostile and rejected when our mate is having a relationship with someone else. Certainly we believe this is one of those cases where resentment is justified and apology and forgiveness would not apply. We feel justified, and we are sure our mate must admit to wrongdoing and ask for mercy. Even if that were to occur, and no matter how much suffering you would want your mate to endure, it may never be enough. Our resentment, once firmly lodged, is not diminished, no matter how much the other person suffers. We are the one who has become transformed by our own resentment, and the only way to release it is to do that work for ourselves. We cannot fix our broken leg by hoping that our mate breaks a leg. Even if our mate does break a leg, that doesn't cure ours. So, even if our anger may be justified, we are harmed by our own resentment. Your anger can be justified and we can still forgive to unhook.

As you are in the process of forgiving you begin to see your spouse in a completely different way. You may see they were a slave to their own pain, that they were powerless over their own actions. For this reason, you have decided this person no longer has power over you, and you begin to see how limited he or she may be. "Limited" is an interesting adjective, as it is not judgmental.

Even if you have done the bookkeeping and have decided that what was done to you is so dreadful, remember forgiveness is not about the other person, who never has to know. There might be conversations with your spouse that may include giving or asking for forgiveness. It is up to you. The forgiveness that I am emphasizing is only for you. As we will discuss, we cannot change the past or past offenses, and holding on to our anger hurts us far more than it hurts the person we are angry with. In addition, forgiveness takes the invective out of the relationship in its own way. With anger dissipated even on just your side, you have changed the recipe and tipped the balance of power in your own favor.

The Gestation Period: From Anger to Forgiveness

If someone puts your hand over a flame, at that moment you will be incapable of thinking your way into not hurting, just as you cannot forgive the flame for burning you. Similarly, during a divorce or separation it is quite difficult to think your way out of anger or even conceive of forgiving the other party. This ball of resentment in your chest may seem like the only thing that is keeping your heart from falling apart. Timing is everything here. You will not be able to accomplish total forgiveness during the tidal wave of your storm, but you will be well rewarded if you make forgiveness your aspiration and your mate your target. At least four stages are required during the gestation period for forgiveness:

1. *In the thick of it:* When someone is really out to harm you and perhaps has the power and means to do so, you clearly will not be ready to forgive. Forgiveness before you are ready is like going into a bull ring without a cape. At this stage it is fine to let your emotions steep and give them room to breathe. Treat them like a flu that has to run its course.

2. *Lingering effects:* You begin to notice how resentment is prevalent in your life, affecting everything you do; it is starting to interfere with your peace and attainment of relief.

3. *Turning point:* You want to do something about the resentment; you no longer want to live like this. Your situation may be excruciating, but you decide to redecorate the swamp even though you are not sure how. If you make forgiveness dependent on your spouse's deserving it, then you have to wait for his or her behavior to change for you to feel better. You are not waiting; you have taken matters into your own hands.

4. *Solution:* You decide to diffuse your spouse's power over you and reframe your story. There is no rule about when it is time to forgive, and there is no objective standard.

When contemplating forgiveness, we need to look dispassionately at our heartache and see what part both parties have contributed. We are not required to discount what the other person has done or to legitimize his or her actions. Our goal is objective reporting. We must consider how much holding on to resentment costs emotionally and even physically. Holding on to resentment has been known to create ulcers and increase anxiety, blood pressure, and body pain. In the act of forgiveness, we can accept that what was done is done; we do not approve of it, we believe it was hurtful, perhaps intentional, but we have chosen to not let the pain remain in our heart or body. We can condemn the act while forgiving the person.

This is counterintuitive, because the thing you want to do the least is what helps you the most and is the fastest exit out of the cycle of resentment and blame. There are other exits out of this cycle—you can disconnect or ignore—but none is as sustaining as forgiveness. With disconnecting or ignoring you must take care to never see or think of the other person. With forgiveness it's all been taken care of—whether or not you ever see or think of the person again.

The antitoxin of forgiveness does not have to be taken right away, and it cannot be force-fed. All you have to do is be open to the possibility, and the inspiration will come when you are ready. The aspiration toward forgiveness does not require forgetting the past or preclude learning from it; it gives you control and power over how you will let the past define who you are in the present and the future.

Is Forgiveness Weakness?

His Holiness the Dalai Lama writes, "When reason ends, anger begins; therefore anger is weakness." Forgiveness does not mean you should not protect yourself against unfairness, abuse, or injustice. You should always take action against unfairness and protect yourself with dignity and calm as soon as you can claim them. There are many ways to protect yourself within and outside the court system, but those methods do not have to be laced with or propelled by resentment and anger. You can be forceful and strong without using anger for fuel. Many people believe that an avalanche of righteous indignation will sweep the judge's decision their way. That is usually not true. What it will do is make the judge run for intellectual cover. The most effective presentation in court is the strong, well-reasoned, and even impassioned one, without the client breathing fire in the background.

Victimhood: A Consensual Crime

With forgiveness—for ourselves and the one we believe has hurt us—we release ourselves from our status as a victim. Seeing yourself as a victim means, "*They* did something to me. I couldn't stop *them*. I have no power over *them*." That soon becomes confused with, "*I* have no power." But when you forgive, you are no longer vulnerable to them; forgiveness gives you back your power. The call is yours as to when you want to diffuse their power.

Your children observe you and model your ability or inability to forgive. Watching you, they can learn to live a life not controlled by resentment. They can observe and internalize the process of forgiveness. The immediate benefit of one parent forgiving the other is that the children's fear of losing the other parent diminishes. Real healing, especially when you have children, is recognizing your interconnectedness with the other parent and learning to navigate that connection.

By the time you are in the middle of your separation or divorce, you usually have a firm story line about what you believe happened in your relationship. You have gone over it in your mind often enough, repeated it to friends and family, possibly even to a lawyer or therapist. You may feel let down by the court system and your attorney or even forsaken by your higher power. You have started to define yourself as the repository of injury and injustice. In fact, a lot of bad things have happened to you, and you may be justified in feeling victimized. After all, remember that the average length of time for a divorce is about two years. Two years of sustained pain can lurk devilishly to fuse "victim" to your new identity.

Usually memory is filtered through our own personal lens, and perhaps our memory needs glasses. After all, we are not highly motivated to rewrite our story line. During separation or divorce, only a part of us really wants to progress or evolve. The other part, often the anchoring part, wants to hold on to the story line, because it may appear to be working for us—that is, until we become more conscious of how that blaming, nonforgiving story line might be hurting us. Even as we become aware that our story line is hurting us, we notice that we are still resistant to change. We believe we are essentially "good"—why shouldn't it be our story line? Why should we re-create it? After all, aren't we the tree, and everyone else the leaves?

Forgiveness understands that everyone is a tree and everyone is a leaf. We are all flawed in some way. To give up our story line requires true crime-scene investigation that vigorously seeks the truth. Can you imagine a different version of why your spouse behaved as he or she did? If not, you might want to look closer at how tightly you hold on to your story line. Think about how you would feel if you could give it up. The situation cannot change, but the way you look at it is your choice when you are determined to become liberated.

With resistance to modifying our story and with repetition, we run the risk of letting these negative thoughts lay down "tracks," forming a brain pattern. The more our brain repeats the story, the more embedded in our thought process it becomes. Other neurons, like good soldiers, will enhance these negative patterns and can translate them into other categories of thought (e.g., "My spouse is out to get me," becomes, "The world is out to get me"). It is as if it were contagious. The idea that we can compartmentalize or isolate negative thoughts about our spouse is perilously untrue. Scientists tell us that it is possible to undo these neuropathways once the tracks have been laid down, but over time it can get more difficult. Dr. Alvaro Pascual-Leone, in describing these habituated tracks, says, "These tracks become really speedy and efficient at getting to their goal."' We have created a negative set point for our thoughts and can quickly gravitate to them. Forgiveness can interrupt this tracking when we allow for a different interpretation or story in which we are no longer the victim.

People often fuse two concepts: that our survival is jeopardized when we are hurt, and that because anger feels powerful it will protect us from this hurt and therefore we can survive. During the divorce we are always looking for strength; we want to feel strong about something, but we often choose to strengthen the wrong thing. We may get angry five times a day, so we are quite familiar with that. But the muscle for forgiveness is quite underdeveloped. The challenge is not to strengthen the anger, but to strengthen the desire for forgiveness.

When you notice that you have slipped into anger to protect yourself, you can unlearn this association. Keeping the anger means that you are emotionally not letting go but are retaining the attachment to your spouse in the neural pathways of your brain. Once you find out you are capable of letting go in a way you didn't know you could, you will have taught your brain (the old dog) new tricks. Any novel way of thinking stimulates your brain and upgrades its clarity.

The barricade that anger creates between us and the other person may feel very desirable. The belief is that separateness is the mental state we need in order to face the termination of the marriage. Blaming is a useful way to maintain separation while telling ourself we are less accountable. And we may be. As we will see later, focusing on weighting the scales of accountability keep us from experiencing the relief that forgiveness can provide.

It is irresistible to blame others and relieve ourselves of responsibility. I am sure that when I bump myself on the table, it is the table's fault. Yesterday I even blamed my table for being messy. It seems to be the easiest way to tolerate life and certainly the injustices delivered by our mate. Blame is for all of us a default position. In the computer world, a default position is the option that will automatically be selected if the user does not select another one. Taking responsibility is harder, because it requires time and effort and self-investigation. Simply put, blame is easier, but ultimately makes us feel worse, because it is the voice of anger. Taking responsibility is harder, but we ultimately feel better. We have a choice.

Forgiveness is understandably not accessible when the froth is still on the beer, but what about ten years later? My friend Susan, who was divorced ten years ago, told me, "I wanted to be detached, and I chose the other way. I pretended he never existed." We talked about the value of just letting resentments continue their slumber. The question came up: Why would you want to open that door you thought you had closed long ago? But the real question is: If you close the door on those demons, does that mean they no longer exist? Psychology has built an entire discipline that says they do exist. To those who say time heals all wounds, I might say that, without purposeful effort, time congeals all wounds. Ironically, this topic came up the night before an amazing thing happened in my courtroom.

I had a case in which for five years a child, Kelly, did not want to see her father. Kelly said her reason was that her father, Kevin, did not come see her when she was away at school. But I was sure there was more to it than that. The mother, Lilly, said she always told Kelly, who was now fifteen, that she should see her father. And yet little progress had been made in changing Kelly's mind, even with therapy. I asked Lilly if she had forgiven her former husband for the pain he caused her. She said, "Absolutely, but I will never forgive him for the pain he caused my child." She gave a righteous and even noble narrative about wanting to protect her child. She then broke down in tears that carried the quality of a fresh wound. Ever since the divorce thirteen years ago, she had carried the weight of her fury strapped to her chest like a baby.

And there it was, the clot in the artery; Lilly's refusal to forgive Kevin had been causing her pain all this time—and she never realized it. She thought her anger had gone into cold storage and was over. It was the first time anyone could see that it was never over. Despite all of the appropriate things she had said to her child ("I want you to visit with your father; I don't want you to hate him"), the child could not repair her relationship with her father, and no one knew why. We now knew. Lilly's anger was still alive and vigorous, and Kelly knew it despite the disguise.

When I asked Kevin if he had ever apologized for the pain he had caused Lilly, after a few minutes he turned to her and said, "I am sorry for any pain I caused you." I watched her soften, but when he started justifying his actions, she tightened, turned away, and resumed her resentful pose. These were the same justifications he gave her thirteen years ago. If she bought into them now, what would have been the purpose of thirteen years of righteous anger? The apology was lost in the shambles of the past. The result was that Lilly still had to hang on to the emotional debt, because justifications, unless they are requested, reinvigorate the offense.

On the surface, no one could argue with a concept that contained the phrase "protect my child." Lilly was sure it was her job to keep the record straight and be the enforcer of moral justice. If she did not hold him to account, who would? She could not let him get away with something unless he admitted to complete wrongdoing. Thirteen years later, he still had not paid the debt of remorse he owed them, and she was going to hold the anger that was the collateral for that unpaid debt. But sadly, no one knew what he could do to pay this debt that would satisfy her, once her resentment had solidified. After all this time, could he ever pay enough? Lilly was never liberated from this agitation, as she made her freedom contingent on his acknowledging his wrongdoings. By not letting him off the hook, she was still on the hook. She was separate from him, but she had not moved on.

I learned so much from this couple when I allowed myself to get in the trenches with them. They are not the only ones who don't forgive—it is all of us, myself included. We all on a daily basis suffer the unfairness and injustices of life, no matter who delivers these injustices: our spouse, our friends, our parents, our children, our country, the universe, or even our higher power. We spend much mental effort on keeping score—who did what to whom and who owes whom. We all believe it is our job to enforce moral justice. It is *not* our job. The laws of karma will take care of that, one way or another, sooner, later, or much later.

Lilly had passed on to her child her system of accounting. She said and believed that it would be disloyal to her daughter if she forgave Kevin. Deep down she knew the legacy she had passed on to her daughter, and she felt that to forgive Kevin now would leave her child bound up in her own resentment. She had taught her daughter how to swim in the cesspool, and now she couldn't just leave her there alone by forgiving her former husband. Lilly thought she had put her emotions in cold storage. But Kelly still felt the heat that prevented her from fully getting on with her life. All this time Lilly thought she was nobly carrying the pain for her daughter, but in reality her daughter was carrying it for her.

The longer we hold on to resentment, the longer we ruminate about the harm done, the more dominant resentment and anger become in our personality. As time goes on, to maintain this dominance, we seek to remember old offenses and look for new ones to keep our current resentment going, so that over time it doesn't lose intensity. Finally, this resentment eclipses our personality, and forgiveness becomes more difficult, as resentment has now become a retaining wall.

Revenge

Many of us believe retaliation is one way to keep power and control. After all, we are right, aren't we? We have been wronged. As we revel in our injustice, we are compelled to experience pain more intensely than the wrongdoer could have ever conceived. But as Confucius said, "Before you embark on a journey of revenge, dig two graves."

Once at a banquet I sat next to a woman who had been divorced eight years. She wasted no time in telling me the agony her husband had caused her. Her anger overripe, she reached fresh exuberance as she told me her husband's new wife was leaving him. She was considering calling the new wife to gift her with ammunition. She said she had been waiting for this for a long time. But anything her husband might have done to her could never have been foul enough to cause the eight years of suffering she had imposed upon herself while waiting for revenge. Had she forgiven him a long time ago, she would not have been entrenched in her need to continue to be a player in his life by becoming a witness to his destruction.

Revenge is the vampire sentiment that keeps you focused only on obtaining fresh blood, rather than the freshness of life. Maybe you hate your spouse. Maybe you would like to see her brought to her knees. But this isn't your job. Life will take of that. It is its nature to do so. But you have a choice, let life take care of it or stay tethered to them, hoping to be the shepherd of his or her destruction.

As you come to understand how you can free yourself from anger and resentment through forgiveness, you will become the creator of your response and therefore the creator of how you feel. When you can think of yourself having the strength to experience forgiveness when you have been wronged, you will no longer be reacting to someone else's injurious behavior. As the creator, you will become empowered. As a reactor you might dread every encounter with your former mate, because you fear what he or she might do to you or the emotions they could stimulate in you. If you have the perspective and nonreactive approach of a creator, that person ultimately could only affect you in ways you allow.

If our attitude is defined by how we are treated externally, by our mate, our children, or the court system, we can only react with an automatic-response pattern that makes us feel we have no choice. Even if we valiantly attempt to not react at all, it often takes just as much stamina. In any event that great an energy connection between us and those we have been wronged by keeps us bound together. Forgiveness is truly an act of self-transformation. It is creative, because it alters the way we relate to the rest of the world. It is freeing, because our reactions are sculpted on our own terms, not theirs.

Your Ex as Inspiration to Transform Your Life?

I often hear, "If only my divorce was over and I didn't have to deal with my spouse all the time, or ever again, my life would be great." It is not only your former mate who is preventing you from being happy and enthusiastic. You may also be preventing your own joy by reacting negatively to his or her behavior.

Many spiritual leaders have told us it is our "enemy" who is our greatest teacher. It is our enemy who inspires us to develop the stronger muscles that are needed for patience, forgiveness, and compassion. The threat offered by our adversary motivates us to do this strenuous spiritual and emotional work. Once we have begun to go to the deeper level of compassion that inspires forgiveness, it will become easier to manage the injustices in everyday life. Each time harm is done to us, it will not stick like flypaper, because we will have experienced the benefits of release. If we have already done the heavy lifting of forgiveness with our former mate, we may now move through other wrongs in our life that have a lighter weight. When we are finally able to do that, and it will not come right away, we will have created a new mechanism for dealing with the many onslaughts of life. We will have learned a different way of looking at the people who have wronged us, knowing we can manage their power over us. We are no longer obstructed by a roadblock whose sentinels remind us of our injuries.

If we are unable to forgive, our spirit is heavy, even if it is resentment against only one person. We think we have compartmentalized that resentment, and it isn't leaking into other relationships. We may be wrong. If we have resentment in us, it could create a barrier between us and everyone else. If resentment lurks, we must judge and separate those who will hurt us and those who will not. We must keep our sensors up at all times as we relate to other people. We don't just build a sensor for one. If we install a burglar-alarm system, it is not just to keep out one person. Everyone is potentially a suspect.

Bathed in the muddy waters of resentment and suspicion it is no wonder we don't have crystal-clear communication with others. By the time you are in the middle of your divorce this muddy water may have become quicksand. Before moving on to the next chapter of your life, consider bathing in the clear water of forgiveness.

Once you build a story line to protect yourself, this pattern becomes entrenched in your brain. You cannot tolerate flexibility as it threatens the protective tissue of your storyline. Perhaps this is the most dangerous thing you could ever do, as it makes your brain less plastic and more rigid. (Plasticity is required for a maximally functioning brain.) All my life experiences tell me forgiveness is the primary strategy. It is the one strategy that can manage all your injuries, from the smallest things to the most gruesome ones; it does not change based on the crime. Forgiveness is the neurological traffic director for injuries to your psyche. It is a way of life. It is not just about your spouse—your spouse is just the exercise. This strategy is for every slight that the world throws at you, whether fate, bad luck, or accidents of birth. Forgiveness is one of the greatest tools for redrawing the neuropathways of your brain.

Transformational Warm-ups

After reading this chapter it would be a very good time to pull out your Personal Manifesto and see if there are any revisions or additions you might consider. Even if you are not ready to forgive, could forgiveness be one of your aspirations?

Unsent Letters

A popular therapeutic exercise is to write a letter when you are angry, but not send it. The purpose of the letter is not its effect on the other person, but to help you begin to express your thoughts and feelings on the issue.

- Write a letter to your spouse or partner listing all the ways you have been hurt and all the reasons you are angry—all of the things you can't or feel you have every right not to forgive.

This first letter can be rambling and furious about why you cannot forgive or perhaps why the other person doesn't deserve it. Feel free to express yourself—the letter will not be sent. Hold on to that letter for a week and reread it. It will start to look like somebody else's ranting. Those feelings you had that were so vehement start to look as vital as old pizza. In the words of musician Thom Yorke, "There is nothing noble in being superior to your fellow man. True nobility is being superior to your former self."

- Write a second letter, again listing the injuries and reasons for anger, but after each one also list some benefits you might receive if you forgave only some of the offenses.

When you rewrite the letter, your level of anger will not be the same.

A portion of a sample first draft of a letter might say:

> I just heard from my lawyer you want a share of the business that I had created before I ever met you. I can't believe you could be so greedy. I am going to stop paying the mortgage and take you off my insurance. No matter what I have done for you, it is never enough, so I might as well stop. I suppose you want my mother's house too. I am telling all of our friends who always say you are "so nice." They need to know the truth.

The second letter might read:

> When I heard that you wanted a share of my business, I felt betrayed. I think you went along with your lawyer, and I know it is their job to ask for as much as they can. I am going to talk to my lawyer about your position, and I want you to know I don't agree and I am told it is not the law. I know the divorce process requires everyone to ask for the moon, but I am not going to do what doesn't seem fair.

Writing about your resentments in a more balanced way, you can observe your process of transformation. As you rewrite the letter, you will notice how emotions can change and resistance to forgive loosens its grip.

I have written letters to former mates and put them in a drawer; when I find them, maybe a year later, I am fairly nauseated by how possessed I was by anger and petty resentments. It seems (almost) impossible that I had written those things. Since the anger and resentment were in my mind only, it is only in my mind that the forgiveness needs to occur.

Do not send any letter to your spouse. But if the urge is irresistible, check with your attorney. The letters are strictly for your own process. Keep them secure or destroy them after you have processed the exercise.

Resentment List

- Make a list of people you resent. The list should include the smallest and the largest offenders. Start thinking about forgiving the ones it would be easiest to forgive—an acquaintance or co-worker perhaps.

This exercise is in the Buddhist tradition. The belief is that as you practice and develop this muscle on the people who are easier to forgive, just as with lifting weights, you are making yourself ready for the harder ones—the heavy lifting. The people you are not ready to forgive yet simply remain on the list for later contemplation. Hold on to forgiveness as an aspiration while keeping in mind the dangers of your anger calcifying into interminable resentment.

- For those you cannot imagine forgiving at this time, write down how you would like to feel about them in the future.

Black-and-White Exercises, or Learning to Love the Gray

I am, you are, everyone—including your spouse—is a collection of contradictions and inconsistencies. At times I can be patient; at times cutting to the chase is way too slow. I have a friend who at times will drop everything to help her friends; at other times, if her friends need something, Scotland Yard couldn't find her. And yet when we are divorcing we often freeze-frame our spouse at his or her worst. In order to gain comfort with the complexities of life, and of people, it is vital to recognize that the key to accepting others' flaws lies in accepting that we all live in the shades of gray.

- Make a list of the five most important people in your life, including yourself, and write down three inconsistencies for each person.

Review this exercise whenever you are angry and disappointed with your former spouse, so you can remember that, although he or she may have been hurtful, you don't want to compound your injury by forgetting that inconsistency is the essence of being human.

Untying the Thoughts That Hold You Hostage

Here is an exercise to help you dissect specific injuries:

- Write down any unkind deed your former spouse has done and answer these three questions about it:

  1. How much time do you spend thinking about the deed? (You may be doing more damage to yourself than your spouse could ever dream up.)

  2. What part of the deed made you angry because it was compounded with other unkind deeds from the past?

  3. What part of the deed activates thoughts of unkind deeds done to you before the marriage by someone else?

Through this crime-scene investigation, you can break down the multiple levels of your reaction and see how much of what was done by your former spouse is muddled by past experiences. This exercise reduces the reactive weight of the offense, puts you in more control of your thought stream, and helps you minimize your offender's power over you.

Forgiveness does not have to be known to its recipient to be effective; apologies, on the other hand, are interactive and can change your relationship to others. Although both forgiveness and apologies are reparative either to you or someone else, in the context of this book neither are dependent upon the reaction of the recipient. You can forgive someone and still not create the trust that apologies can. You can apologize to someone and never touch the spot in your heart that has to do with forgiveness. Although saying you're sorry can be a soul-cleansing activity, in the next chapter you will see how it not only redefines your relationship to other people, but is also an unexpected power strategy.

8

Apologies

Managing the Ebb and Flow of Trust

An apology might help, but you can change your life without one.
—ROBIN QUIVERS

In a culture of drive-by relationships and what sometimes seems like fast-food communication, we sometimes can leave people and situations we have handled unskillfully behind, like a used Kleenex. Why apologize when our transgressions are small and we may never see the people again? In the case of divorce and separation, why apologize when the other's crimes were felonies, and ours were only misdemeanors?

The act of apology is a highly effective technique for dealing with conflict situations. It serves us and it lubricates our interactions with others equally. My definition of an apology in this chapter does not necessarily include asking for forgiveness or forgiving others. The act of making apology is merely a way of taking responsibility for a harm we may have inflicted on another.

Your reflexive response may be, "Why would I apologize to someone who left me without good reason, broke up our family, and refuses even to talk about it?" Perhaps you've dug your heels in on this one: "Apologize? Never!" Yes, nature creates hurricanes and tsunamis that wipe away people and cities, but isn't love the one thing that's supposed to last? How are you supposed to apologize to your mate who has forced you to change your belief in eternal love? If your answer is, "When hell freezes over!" consider how much energy you need to burn to keep those fires going.

I have asked many people to tell me the first word that comes to mind when they feel they have something to apologize for. The answers were consistently "sad" or "embarrassed." "It rolls around in my head for days, and I am afraid to see the person," one friend admitted. The absence of apology is a cry from the silent space that forms after the offense has happened and continues to echo until the apologies are made.

There is a tendency to evaluate whether our former partner deserves an apology by using his or her past behavior as a gauge rather than evaluating our own imperfect behavior. The belief is that if we admit to having placed one faulty brick where we are to blame in our constructed story line, then the foundation of our entire story line may be at risk. We fear that the admission of even one incident of unskilled behavior on our part will allow our former partner to interpret that as an admission of many other wrongdoings.

Consider the possibility that if you are repeating your story over and over to your friends, family, lawyer, or therapist and not getting any relief from it, maybe something is missing in your story. Relief is available through a more objective accounting in which you include rather than exclude your own accountability. Apologies can be painful in the anticipation of their execution, but they can give years of enduring relief. Demanding to be correct, or justifying your conduct and therefore not apologizing, is not where the power lies. The power lies in being willing to be open to other versions of any difficult situation.

Why Taking Responsibility Gives You Power

A rigid conviction that you would never apologize to a person who had harmed you hinders the possibility of your taking any responsibility in a situation. When you take some responsibility (however minor) for your actions, you loosen the grip that being a victim of someone else's behavior may have on you. As that person loses power, you assume greater control. You might think the opposite is true—that the wrongdoer has all the power. Unfortunately, this causes you to adopt a victimlike perspective. "Look what he did to me!" or "Look how she hurt me!" you assert, as if this is the only accurate description of the incident. With those kinds of thoughts, you give your former mate quite a bit of power, because you believe he or she can hurt you anytime, and has.

My friend Mandy told me, "We don't want to apologize because we don't want to be wrong or admit that we are wrong." When we think of our difficult histories and the defenses we have built up over the years, how is it possible that we haven't been wrong somewhere, at some point? We all worry about losing credibility when we admit we are wrong, but with apologies we actually gain credibility. Consider how you feel when someone apologizes to you and takes responsibility. You think to yourself, "Now there is someone I might trust." On those occasions when you have apologized, you notice that it is contagious. When the dialogue opens up, you often find that the issue was one of miscommunication.

Two Completely Different Reasons for Apologies

You do not have to want to maintain the relationship in order to apologize. Nor do you have to care about the other person's reaction to benefit from apologizing. There are a least two reasons for apologizing.

- To grease the skids of the relationship and to build trust, whether just for the two of you or because of the interactions you will have if you have children.
- To allow yourself to detach from the relationship completely and with dignity by owning up to whatever you did; this results in a clean break without residual attachment.

In a previous chapter I proposed a definition of forgiveness that cleans up the landscape and releases the person who is forgiven to his or her fate, without your help. With apologies, the dynamics are slightly different. With a simple but sincere "I'm sorry," you cut the cord of responsibility in a situation that has kept you tied to the other person. Now you are free to detach or to construct a new, positive interaction untainted by the destructive routines of the past.

Some people enjoy not apologizing. It is a small way to take a mini-revenge. It means, "That's my action, and I am sticking to it. If I apologize, I would have to give up my anger, which I am not ready to do." If this is you, even as you say the words "sticking to it," it becomes clear that you have chosen not to free yourself. Even if you are not ready to give up your anger now, consider the benefits that will be all yours when you are ready to avail yourself of them.

Apologies: So Powerful They Are Almost Machiavellian

People believe they are giving up power when they apologize. Actually, however, they are getting it. If you apologize, it feels to the receiver as though you are detaching from the fray. You are saying, "I am no longer in the game." If the other person wants to continue to interact with you, the only thing left for that person to do is to reach a higher level with you that is not about rehashing your old offenses. It is unnerving to the other person to see you are no longer vested in having to be right or having to present a perfect front. Intuitively that person knows you are somehow removing yourself from the negative cycle. That is when you begin getting the power. As my friend Jackie puts it, "The way to win the tug of war is to let go of the rope."

You also feel more powerful when you apologize, because when you act benevolently, instinctively you like yourself better. The person you apologize to instinctively knows you hold the key to your own freedom. You have taken your part of the responsibility, and there is little the other can do to you. You are now out of reach. It is devastating to the other person if you are detached enough to apologize. You may think apologizing is a sign of weakness. As described here—and in its effect on your life—it is clearly not a weakness.

After reading this chapter, Carol apologized to her former husband for her past wrongs—fifteen years after their divorce. She did it to make sure he came to their son's wedding, but she got the unexpected surprise of having the best conversation she had had with him in years. Her motives may have been based on self-interest, but she found that he responded to her in a completely different way. Once she apologized and once he realized she was no longer participating in the negative cycle, they decided they did have something left together: the joy of their son's wedding.

Maybe you are not ready for a clean break. If you don't apologize and your former mate is still angry with you, you are still in his or her life. Is that how you want to be in someone's life? As long as you know that you should apologize and it is still on your mind, however infrequently, it remains sticky, unfinished business. When I see people fighting hard in court, I know they are looking for something they don't even know they are looking for. They are looking for an acknowledgment of the injustices, which includes giving and getting apologies. By the time the court process has finished bruising them, they will have both wished they had apologized to begin with.

What Makes an Apology Warranted?

Apologizing is not contingent on whether your spouse has earned an apology, but on whether you want to take responsibility for your part in any of the problematic scenario. This is not self-blame, but an opportunity for self-honesty. This is not acceptance or forgiveness of another person's faulty behavior; it is an incredible way to get your power back. In the tangled sequence of who did what to whom, when you take responsibility for your part and then apologize, you begin to trust your own actions and to gain trust from a source in whom it has become scarce—your spouse. Here are examples of apologies you could make no matter how much blame your spouse might have in the big picture:

"I am sorry I was very critical of your family."

"I am sorry I ignored you and that my first priority appeared to be work."

"I am sorry my spending harmed our family."

Remember, these apologies do not justify the behavior of the other person, and they are not meant to. They are only meant to show you that the other person does not have to earn an apology; it only matters what you want to do for yourself.

If we decide to measure our actions by how right or wrong the other person is, during a divorce we would probably never see anything we could take responsibility for, because we are too hurt by even the slightest offense. That is how raw we are during divorce. Our challenge is to not be so dominated by our pain that we can't release ourselves from our guilt about our harmful behavior.

If you decide to stay in your pain, locked into endless thoughts of everything your spouse has done to harm you, you will tread a circular path. This path will always provide plenty of good reasons not to take responsibility. It's as if your spouse stole a million dollars from you. Perhaps you only stole a dollar from your spouse. The size of the theft doesn't matter. If you took the dollar, own up to it, even if there is no retribution for the greater theft by your spouse. Why shouldn't you get the full benefits of clearing your karma, even if your harmful acts were insignificant?

The Difference Between Apologies and Forgiveness

Do you have to forgive to apologize? No. Do you have to forgive to accept an apology? Again, no. You only have to thank your partner for acknowledging his or her part in the situation. It is only an apology. You are not absolving him or her of wrongdoing, nor, when you apologize, are you requesting absolution for your wrongdoing.

If you are willing to listen to an apology, will that be interpreted as letting someone off the hook completely? No. You can say, "I accept your apology for taking money out of the account, but I still insist it be returned." This statement acknowledges a past action, but says nothing about you altering a justified position.

Are you obligated to accept an apology? No. You can think it over and get back to the person or say you are not ready to accept. What does it mean if you don't accept? You may be harming yourself, and you may not get any more apologies in the future. However, it may take time to process apologies. The offenses that have occurred seem to have resulted in a severe consequence—the breakdown of your marriage. It is as if two gladiators were fighting and one said, "Oops, I'm sorry that I stabbed you in the heart." Sometimes the best you can do is ask for time to think it over or just say, "I appreciate your having said that. I may have a lot more healing to do before I can accept."

Both apologies and forgiveness involve the same issue: your energies are tied up in the other person. If I have wronged you and have not apologized, my energy is still wrapped up with you. Apologies and forgiveness are vehicles that move energy out of a stagnant, negative state and remodel your connection with another person, even if it is detachment. Our unfinished business keeps our energy bound up with those issues, and when that unfinished business is negative, we set ourselves up for an unending drain on our emotional energy. Anger and resentment drain the psyche and emotional reserves. Forgiveness and apology mark the route toward ending these negative energy patterns and offer us a way of keeping severe energy depletion from becoming a chronic emotional state.

When you decline to forgive, you might hold on to the accompanying resentment in perpetuity. When you hold on to that sentiment, you block the movement of energy. The energy of anger and resentment must shift, because blocked energy creates emotional sludge, which can prevent you from moving forward. Ask yourself what happens when a lane of traffic is blocked. Something has to give, and in the realm of emotional interaction, apologies and forgiveness clear the blockage. When you try it, with all the beauty of its difficulty, you will notice that there has been some movement in your psyche.

Granting forgiveness or offering an apology really has little to do with the other person involved. The practice of these two energy-management techniques enables you to determine who gets your energy and who doesn't. In a sense, this means you actually decide who has power over you and who doesn't. When you call your own energy back to yourself by refusing to let it linger over wrongs between you and another, regardless of who is at fault, you take positive steps to separate your energy from that of the other person. You're not letting anyone off the hook; you're letting go of the hook altogether.

When we apologize or forgive, we are not giving up anything except wasted emotion. If we hold on to resentment, we fool ourselves into thinking we are keeping ourselves safe, that we are protecting ourselves from being hurt again. In reality, we are sentencing ourselves to a life that is less satisfying because it is encumbered with unfinished business.

Barren Apologies: Offering a Cookie Jar with No Cookies

The great non-apology was given by President Richard Nixon when he left office in 1974: "I regret deeply any injuries that may have been done in the course of the events that led to this decision. I would say only that if some of my judgments were wrong, and if some were wrong, they were made in what I believed at the time to be in the best interest of the nation."

He did not take responsibility for any specific wrong. He said some of his judgments were wrong, but we really don't know what he was apologizing for. He could have been apologizing for choosing the wrong color towels for the washroom in the Oval Office. We are not even certain if there are any wrongs. This was not an apology, but an excuse. He was excusing himself "in the best interest of the nation," letting himself off the hook for any wrong done.

Here are examples of other forms of apology that may also be ineffective:

"I am sorry if you thought that any harm was done to you." The inference here is that the injured party is unusually fragile, has misperceived something, and is difficult to communicate with. This apology implies that people of normal sensibilities might not have been harmed, and that the injured party may therefore not be normal.

"I am sorry I hurt your feelings, but I would never have done it if you hadn't brought up the issue of finances." This makes the injured party the instigator and therefore the one responsible for bringing the injury upon him- or herself.

"I am sorry if I have done anything to hurt you." This apology does not acknowledge the wrong done; the "if" says the speaker thinks there might not have been any injury at all. The injured party cannot feel that the speaker is really apologizing for the hurt; the speaker doesn't appear to even know what the injury was, but just wants the conflict to be over.

"I am sorry. I know I have injured you. I can see you've lost a lot of weight and don't sleep well. But I have developed ulcers from the situation as well." This apology calls attention to the speaker's pain, which diminishes the apology. This appeal for sympathy makes the apology the platform for complaining about the injured party's behavior; the apology has become about the speaker, not the injured party.

Any apology made by rote in a flat, unaffected tone, this does not convey true regret. An apology given with about as much emotion as a tollgate worker waving a car through has about as much value as the quarter tossed at the basket.

Any apology with the words "because," "the reason is," or "but" in it. This is a false apology used as an opportunity to justify the actions.

Open Sesame: Apologies That Open the Heart

An effective apology has an emotional component demonstrating that the party actually feels sorry: "I feel terrible that I did that," or, "It is hard to express how badly I feel." An effective apology offers no excuse or defense: "I am sorry I came late to get the children, I am sorry this made you late for your appointment."

A qualified apology is less than effective: "I am sorry I came home late so often, but I was working hard for the family." That may very well be true, but the excuse does not belong in the apology. It belongs in a different conversation. This person should offer only the apology, but may add, "If you would like to hear more about why I behaved as I did, I would love to have that conversation with you." That discussion should be kept separate.

An effective apology does not depend on whether it is accepted. If you have gone so far as to gather up the courage and wisdom to apologize, don't undo it by reacting negatively to a rejection of your apology. The listener may store your apology in order to contemplate it later, out of your presence. Sometimes the listener will never even bring it up again, but you might notice a difference in his or her conduct.

Some components of an effective apology include:

- Acknowledging the importance of your relationship with the other person: "You are the mother of our child, and I want our relationship to continue to be amicable. It means a lot to me that you accept my apology."
- Offering to make it up to the injured party: "I agree with you. I did speak to you critically in front of the children. I was frustrated and took it out on you. You didn't deserve that. Next time I am going to go out of my way to be respectful and kind."
- For repeated apologies, include why it is different this time and some insight into past behavior: "I know I have apologized before, and yet I continue to be late. I guess I have just realized how this upsets your entire schedule and how selfish I have been. I just never looked at it that way before."

In some cases, there is no obvious way to make up for an injury. For example, if it is your fault that the other party missed a vacation with the children, it may be impossible to "redo" the vacation. But you can ask, "Is there anything I can do to make this up to you?" There may be a request that you can fulfill, showing your good faith.

In those cases where it is truly impossible to make it up to a person, it is still important that your apology acknowledge the injury, rather than glossing over it as if it didn't happen. In so many divorce cases, one party feels more strongly that the other was the cause of the divorce. When this is true, the lack of acknowledgment to the injured party by the mate is one reason cases end up going to trial. The wronged party's damage has not been acknowledged, and he or she wants to use the court system to make the other party repent. If the damaging party doesn't give that acknowledgment, the mistaken belief is that the court system, including the judge, will exact retribution.

"Will She Use It Against Me in Court?"— Apologies and the Courtroom

As you consider apologizing, you may say to yourself: "I probably could apologize for some things I did, but I certainly can't do it after what my spouse did in court the other day. Especially when I think about the money this divorce is costing our family, money we could've used to pay debts or our daughter's college tuition."

Apologizing under such circumstances may seem to you like the Titanic apologizing to the iceberg. By the time people are in the heat of a divorce battle, everybody's behavior is so reactive it is impossible to tell who is offending and who is reacting. Nor does it matter. Apologies put the brakes on the chain reaction. I have rarely seen a situation in which one of the parties had not contributed to the breakdown of the relationship. Yes, I have seen situations in which one party's wrongdoing was more apparent, where the behavior was worse—sometimes despicable. But rarely have I seen a situation in which one person had no culpability at all.

We have all known people who absolutely cannot apologize, because it makes them feel too vulnerable. I had a case in which I asked a woman to write out the apology she wanted to hear from her soon-to-be former husband. I asked her to write it as if he were writing it. I told her to give it to him and ask him if he would sign it. He either cannot formulate it or say it out loud, but to my amazement, I was told he signed it right away.

Often people think apologies mean they are guilty of wrongdoing, and they believe they might look bad to the court. The adversarial system does not have an atmosphere that promotes apology, because nobody wants to admit fault in front of the court or the other lawyer.

Despite that, I can pretty much guarantee that an apology is looked upon with respect in court. This, of course, does not include those cases where an admission of wrong would jeopardize somebody's legal position.

Unfortunately, lawyers are not usually trained to instruct their clients in the efficacy of sincere remorse and regret. Few would even recommend this as a strategy. However, this may be changing. Johns Hopkins University has now established formal apology practices and procedures to minimize hostility in malpractice suits. Studies have shown that when doctors have greater communication with their patients and apologize for their mistakes, their patients are less likely to sue. If the medical world can move in this direction, let us hope the legal world is not far behind.

A sincere and well-crafted apology can exert a profound effect upon the injured party. This person, who previously felt attacked, even besieged, may feel a sense of power arising from the ability to accept or reject an apology. Given the opportunity, most people like to see themselves as benevolent, and gracious acceptance of a sincere apology can provide powerful and much-needed validation for a person who feels injured. For the injured party, such an apology signifies respect, and when respect is maintained, the behavioral bar is raised for all parties to the process. In fact, I have rarely seen a case go to trial in which the divorcing spouses have maintained baseline levels of respect and civility.

It would be hard to imagine a marriage in which the partners have nothing to apologize for. In the same way that an actor in a Broadway performance cannot take all the credit when the performance is good, neither can one person in a relationship absorb all of the blame. Judges know that both parties have contributed to the breakdown. Most judges believe that taking responsibility for unskilled behavior is respectable, if not admirable.

A caveat is in order here, however. Apologies that occur too late in the divorce process may appear insincere. In fact, an apology proffered during or after a breakdown of negotiations or worse, to break a deadlock, will almost assuredly be subject to skepticism. But a sincere apology, even a belated one, is almost never lacking value.

One day during a trial in my courtroom, after days of fighting for his continued possession and control of the family scrap-metal business, during cross-examination the husband broke down crying. Desperate and willing to try anything, he apologized to his wife for all the years he had put the business ahead of the family. He acknowledged that she had done most of the work raising the children and that she had done a great job. Despite the lateness of the gesture, the apparent insincerity of his motives, and the circumstances under which it was made, something in his voice changed. Suddenly his wife, whom he had always made to feel needy and possessive when she complained about his long hours, felt that her pain and suffering were finally being recognized and validated. Although she had been cautioned that this was a manipulation, her anger decreased almost instantly upon hearing his apology. The act of apologizing affected the husband as well. Even if it started out contrived, he was still processing it. I have found in court that if people don't mean to apologize, they simply can't do it. Ultimately, the couple worked out a fair division of their assets, and this was possible only because the defining anger in their relationship had been defused because he took responsibility for his part in the demise of the marriage.

Certified Justice Accountant (CJA)

If you are an accountant by nature, keeping records of who you have offended or who has offended you, and employ the concept of "due and owing" in your personal relationships, consider the following: Write the check (apologize), and date the check ("I am sorry I hung up on you this morning"). The sooner you deliver the apology, the less resentment interest you will accumulate. You no longer have to give mental attention to who owes you what, what you did wrong, who you owe, etc. On an ongoing basis, you have balanced your interpersonal checkbook, and that balance becomes available to you with a single sentence: "I'm sorry."

The Right Atmosphere for Apologies

Studies have shown that the most effective learning takes place in an atmosphere conducive to learning. Similarly, people only really hear what we have to say when they are feeling receptive. Experts agree that the atmosphere most conducive to learning and accepting information occurs when the listener is having a positive experience.

If you want to get a point across that is important to you, you should not do it during a heated argument or a time of festering resentment. Given the fact that divorce is by its very nature a negative time, it is helpful to create pockets of softness where your spouse can hear information and requests. Delivering an apology creates one of those pockets.

An example would be your husband's picking up the children for visitation. If you want him to remember to give your child his medicine, instead of reminding him that he forgot the last time and telling him he has been irresponsible about taking care of details during visitation, you must create a positive environment for listening. You might say: "Eddie had such a good time last time he was with you; he is very excited about going bowling. Here is the medicine he needs to take, and it really is very important, so please help him and make sure he gets it. I'm sorry that I yelled at you last Wednesday about the medicine."

Apologizing to Your Child

I have noticed a consistent theme in what children tell me when I talk with them privately with their lawyer. Children in their candor reveal how important they think apologies are. Perhaps the most horrific example was a case involving two children who were physically punished by their father if they did not hit their mother when they were with her. Seven years after the divorce became final, the father was seeking to expand his visitation time.

When I spoke with the children to ascertain their feelings about it, the two boys were adamant about not wanting to see him. The younger one's eyes filled with tears; the older one, age fourteen, was angry at even being asked to see his father. However, despite the unmistakable negative response, both boys made a point of saying that things might have been different if their father had ever apologized to them for his abusive and manipulative behavior.

Transformational Warm-ups

Just reading this chapter is not enough. Be willing to give apology a try, and you will find the magic.

- Practice apologizing to those who are not key to your life. Let's say you get mad at a taxi driver because you are in a rush and you over-react about the route taken. Apologize for overreacting. See how it feels. I recommend starting in small increments, warming up that muscle before you use it with that person to whom it is most difficult for you to apologize.
- Make a list of times you have been deeply wronged by your spouse, and next to each one write down any part of the situation that re-sulted because you had done something wrong (perhaps you even instigated it).
- Ask your spouse what he or she likes to hear in an apology. Ask for the dialogue your spouse will be receptive to. Many times we apol-ogize, but we don't use the code language another can hear and be receptive to.

Part Two laid out the array of possible minefields arising from the divorcing process and offered guidance for managing and minimiz-ing their effects. In Part Three we discuss how those minefields might impact your children and how to prevent collateral damage. The good news is that there are real solutions and clear direction to minimize the effect of divorce on children.

PART THREE
PREVENTING COLLATERAL DAMAGE

9

Damage to Children

Developing the Heroic in Your Parenting

Let me give you one definition of ethics: it is good to maintain life
and to further life; it is bad to damage and destroy life. And this
ethic, profound, universal, has the significance of religion. It is
religion.
—ALBERT SCHWEITZER

I love my children. I would never do anything to hurt them," say
parents. Operating under the illusion that love conquers all,
most parents overwhelmingly believe that whatever behavior
they engage in during their divorce, their children will get over it in
the long run. The belief in this myth appears to give parents license
to behave any way their urges dictate. It is almost as if being in pain
means they can break the rules.

This belief is at least part of the reason that children coming from
those families that make up the 50 percent divorce rate have been negatively and indelibly stamped. The results of long-term studies of children of divorce done by Dr. Judith Wallenstein, author of *The Unexpected
Legacy of Divorce,* have shown that, as adults, two out of three children
of divorce decide not to have children of their own. The reasons given
range from: they would not want to be the kind of parent they had, to
they would not know how to parent and thought they would have little

talent for it, to if their marriage ended in divorce their children might go through the same horrible experience they had.[1]

I call this an epidemic, because according to this research a primary reason for marriage (to have children) no longer exists as it did in the past. What is wrong with this picture? Can it be true that so many children are being so damaged when their parents often mean so well? I began to search for the disconnect between parents' hearts and their behavior that could account for this disturbing trend.

I started my search by asking a husband who had admitted to hitting his wife in front of their children if he understood why this was so damaging to them. He answered candidly that, no, he really didn't know why that would harm his children, because he wasn't hitting them. Although that may have been an extreme example of parental obliviousness, it got me thinking.

I continued to ask litigants battling in (and out of) my courtroom if they thought that arguing in front of their children or speaking negatively about their spouse was damaging. Some parents thought those actions might be damaging, but few could articulate the dangers. The truth is, too many weren't really sure, or they didn't exactly know how those actions could be damaging. I've come to understand the importance of spelling out the dire correlation between their combative spousal conduct and damage to their children. I tried to determine what the most damaging pervasive myths are that parents believe. The frightening answers are what led to this book. It all started with the children.

Three Blind Myths

Although there are exceptions, it is rare for a parent to actually want to intentionally injure or endanger a child. When asked, most parents emphatically say that they live to protect their children. Their belief is profoundly felt, but often inconsistent with their behavior. The axis of carelessness where children are harmed is usually located at the intersection of good intentions and unskilled behavior. This chapter and the two that follow it are difficult on the heart, but they are important in the same way an MRI is crucial to identifying a physical problem.

You might not want to know a problem is lurking, but if you don't find out about it, you will never have the opportunity to make it better.

For most parents, protection takes on a decidedly physical nature. They are diligent about sheltering their children from physical danger, teaching them to look both ways before they cross the street, and buckling them into protective car seats. This diligence extends to other dangers as well. Parents are careful to shelter their children's sense of self-esteem and emotional health. They may limit their exposure to violent TV and pay close attention to their interactions with friends and siblings. Mindful parents practice constructive criticism, attempting to separate the behavior from the child, so that misbehavior can be corrected without traumatizing the child's psyche. And then along comes Divorce Vader, delivering you into darkness.

One of the side effects of divorce for parents is the development of a compensating blind spot in their psychological rearview mirrors. This blind spot obscures the truth that very loving parents do unintentional damage to their children. Divorcing parents may become so depleted just trying to think and function that they are unable to supply, or even comprehend, the amount of extra nurturing their children need. Thus the blind spot serves a useful function—to obscure the children's fragility while they focus on their own survival. But parents need to be superskilled in detecting, and avoiding, unintentional psychological damage to their children caused by the divorcing process. They need to engage in heroic parenting.

Humpty Dumpty: The Myth of Resiliency

The myth that children are resilient is conventional wisdom that is overrelied upon to the serious detriment of children of divorce. The notion that children will just get over it eventually and that the cumulative hurt of the divorce period will be washed away like footprints in the sand contributes to a false sense of security.

Children get taller, they pass on to the next grade, they continue to mature—and we interpret this as resiliency. That children have "survived" a divorce is no indication they are thriving emotionally. The internal turmoil these children experience does not match the outward evidence of healthy, growing children. According to Vietnamese Buddhist monk Thich Nhat Hanh, children, like flowers, cannot survive independently. He explained that they are completely dependent upon the soil in which they are planted, the sunlight they receive, and the rain that waters them.[2]

Children of divorce are often planted in soil contaminated by anger or depleted of vitality through depression. The sunlight they need may be occluded by a dark cloud that covers the hearts of the parents. The precipitation they receive may be tears of acid rain, carrying unfiltered chemical deposits from a sky polluted by the ashes of their parents' dreams. Resiliency can and will occur, but it must be fostered through heroic parenting; it cannot be left to chance.

Sleeping Beauty: The Myth of Memory

Another frightening myth is that children are somehow sleeping through the whole divorce and will forget the behavior they have seen. They will forget a lot, but not enough.

I always believed that the myth about children forgetting was true for my son. I see things differently now, since my adult son recently told me he could recall words and phrases from arguments I had with his father before, during, and after our divorce. He told me he was terrified and even feared we wanted to get rid of him, because we always seemed to be arguing about him. He quoted to me these conversations in vivid detail. It was not a joyous memory for my son, my former husband, or me, and it was a startling revelation for me, since I thought our divorce was quite civil. He was only four years old at the time.

Malice in Kinderland: The Danger of Free Speech

When you look at your child, what do you see? Does she have blonde hair, brown eyes? Is he tall or short? Can you see beyond the physical body to really know who your child is? Consider your child as a mass of cells and energy. Those cells were created by you and your spouse. When a marriage dissolves, there's often a great desire to dissociate your spouse's cells from your child. When relationships terminate, people usually make a list of indictments rather than endearments that include the negative aspects of the other spouse as a parent. Attempts may be made to corrode and devalue the child's connection with the other parent. No matter how much you might want to dissociate your spouse's cells from your child, when you lie to yourself about the importance of the other parent, you start to trump reality with your desired perception. You look for incidents to support the devaluation of your former mate. Soon your child doesn't know what to believe. Although your version may not ring true, your child loves you, so he or she wants to accept your interpretation of truth. It becomes difficult for your child to distinguish truth from shades of truth and shades of falsehood, because your child's internal calibrating mechanism, which is in its formative stages, has been skewed.

Your child knows he or she is a combination of Mommy and Daddy. When you hate your spouse, a child thinks you hate that part of him or her as well. By destroying the child's loving attachment to one parent, you interrupt the child's intrinsic need to feel confident that he or she will be well taken care of by that parent. The safer and stronger each parent appears to the child, the more secure your child will feel. The question that should be foremost in your mind is whether you want one of your child's main protectors to be perceived by that child as ineffectual, damaged, or incompetent because of your hostility or criticism. Ask yourself how that would make your child feel. Your top agenda should be to make sure that the spouse who is caring for your child feels as good as possible so he or she will have the resources and energy to give the best care, and that your child's perception of the other parent is one that enables the child to feel safe, comfortable, and protected.

In my courtroom I have heard parents say, "I believe my child should know the real truth." This statement is usually delivered as if the parent is addressing an audience on behalf of a righteous cause sponsored by the Society for the Preservation of the Truth. Philosopher Blaise Pascal puts it well when he writes, "The abuse of truth ought to be as much punished as the introduction of falsehood." So I ask the truth teller, "Which do you think is more important, that your child knows the truth as you see it, or that your child is happy?"

In the name of truth, one parent is attempting to erode the child's positive attachment to the other parent. If the maligning parent is successful, grinding down the bond between the child and the other parent, it is viewed as a victory. But, instead, what the maligning parent may have succeeded at is destroying that child's ability to have positive attachments later in life. In an environment in which the child feels she can only be loved by adopting one parent's reality, the child learns that love is conditional. Later in life, in relationships, this impinges on the child's ability to have her needs met if it conflicts with what her mate wants. She must go along with what her mate wants in order to get love.

One day in court, a mother was seeking an increase in child support from her former husband. The father testified that his income had declined dramatically. After the case was over, I was riding down the elevator with the mother and the parties' teenage daughter. They did not notice I was there or did not recognize me out of my black robe. The mother was sharing details of the case with the daughter, as I would not let the daughter come into the courtroom. The mother was telling her what a liar and manipulator her father was, fully expecting the daughter to agree. I knew there was no way this child would ever be able to hear her father's side of the story. Even if the father was lying, I wondered why the mother could not share her frustration with her sister, her neighbor, or even the cashier at the corner store. Anyone but the child.

I was saddened, because I knew that sharing this information with the daughter might forever affect the way the girl viewed her father and ultimately how she viewed men in general. Would they all be liars and manipulators to her? The daughter had no way to defend her trust in her father against this onslaught; she would certainly question it and probably cease to rely on it. Could the mother be sure the daughter would heal from believing that her father is manipulative, uncaring, and a liar? I don't believe the mother considered the long-term effects. If she had, I don't think she would have intentionally hurt her daughter.

This is an example of the prevalent disconnect between the actions and the consequences of the actions of a parent who probably does love the child. As a parent, what would you think of a teacher who taught your child hate and animosity under the guise of a justified cause? Would you let your child go to that school?

There is another kind of maligning that is as subtle as a gentle breeze of nerve gas. This potent style of denigration sounds like this: "Go ask your father for the money for your prom dress; he has much more money than I do." Or, "Ask your mom to give you the soccer money. That's what I give her child support for." When the children's requests are not met, this is a sure-fire way to raise doubt in their minds about the other parent's affection. The manipulating parent knows what the outcome is going to be and executes the maneuver like a hangman. This passive-aggressive behavior sets the other parent up as "non-giving" or "non-caring" in the child's mind.

Though the parent who deftly hangs the blame on the other parent feels like a victor, everyone loses here. The other parent is cast as un-caring. From the child's view it looks as though money was given to the other parent for the child's benefit, but the other parent chooses not to spend it on the child. The child goes without the prom dress or the soccer gear and blames it on the parent who withheld the money. These are ways children learn to connect money with love, and to connect not receiving money with being unloved. The lesson the parent imparts is that money buys feelings and affection. For most, this is a character deal-breaker.

Eeny, Meeny, Miny, Moe: Children Choosing Sides

In a divorce campaign, the children, especially teenagers, often feel they have to take sides. Lining up against one parent in favor of the other eventually may affect the child's self-esteem as he or she approaches the teenage years and adulthood. They may dislike themselves or feel guilty for that breach of loyalty to the other parent. Choosing differ-ent sides can break up siblings' attachment to each other as well. When siblings are force-fed different editorialized party lines, they may be cast into warring enemy camps. In this complicitous dance, the chil-dren gauge which side is buttering their bread. Meanwhile, children learn they have newfound power and importance. Mutual manipula-tion becomes the mode of behavior in this scenario.

Chicken Little: Chilling Consequences Confirmed

Another prevalent fiction is that the only time children are damaged is during the actual divorce proceedings. However, statistics show that in both contested and uncontested cases, many parents remain angry with each other long after the divorce proceedings are over. One-third of the couples in Dr. Judith Wallenstein's studies were still fighting feverishly ten years after their divorce, resulting in continual damage to the children.[3] The feelings of hurt and humiliation, plus fights over child support and visitation, continue long after the papers are signed. In the midst of all the unresolved issues, the entry of a potential new partner for either of the parents usually fires up the old anger. It is true that emotions can soften, but when there is a great deal of anger and resentment, it can incubate and increase over the years. The original unresolved issues are brought to the table every time the parties have an encounter with each other.

We have become accustomed to living in a polluted environment. Similarly some have come to accept that damage might be done to children in the process of a divorce and that this might be especially true in a high-conflict divorce. But many parents don't discuss how their behavior affects their children. As a matter of fact, many parents try to put the whole issue of what is happening to the children in a box, to be locked away as soon as possible. What happened during the divorce, and the reasons for the divorce, are often not talked about again. Once that box has been locked, a secret society develops in each household between the parent and the children. A silent vow is taken to not talk about the children's ongoing fears. Families can go on this way year after year, and the illusion persists that everything is fine.

London Bridge Is Falling Down: Depleted Parent Syndrome

"Depleted parent syndrome" is not a medically recognized condition. As a matter of fact, you will not read about it in any other book. But you certainly know when you have it: at the time your child most needs your energy, optimism, and support and is watching you closely for signs that everything is going to be all right, you find yourself unable to satisfy those needs.

As a loving parent, watching your children suffer can trigger a great amount of guilt, which may further deplete your crucially needed resources. Guilt is a destructive emotion that not only diminishes your energy, but can cause you to feel defensive toward the people around you, including your children. For example, if it is suggested you should stay home more with your child, you might immediately respond, "But I never miss a soccer game." The point is you are starting to block out information that pushes the guilt button. As you start developing these defenses, you may become hypersensitive and drive people away.

In this chapter the focus was on the perspective of the parents during the divorcing process. In the next chapter we turn to the perspective of the children. If children could articulate their feelings, this is what they would say.

10

Your Child's Wounded World

During a divorce, parents' and children's needs are out of sync. It is not that parents love their children less than before, but they are preoccupied with the rebuilding of their entire life. In some ways the children are left to fend for themselves emotionally. They watch vigilantly for times when their parents might be available to provide a drop of the old nectar of normalcy. When I see angry or stressed parents battling each other in my courtroom, I can't imagine where they will find the emotional reserves to support their children.

When an adult is suffering from depleted parent syndrome, children feel they have lost part of the parent they knew, the part that has succumbed to the demons of anger, depression, and frustration. Children usually cannot articulate what is missing from the parent they were used to—they just know something is different. The parents are at their soccer games and recitals, they make them dinner, but something is missing. Children usually do not have the ability to separate themselves from their parents; if their parents are suffering it means that they, the children, may have done something "wrong." These children can't put their finger on it, but like a missing limb that still hurts, they suffer the loss of the parent they knew and compensate with an emotional limp.

No matter how smart your children may be, they have a limited ability to understand what is happening during this difficult time. Developmentally, younger children see themselves as responsible for most events in their lives. They don't see things in terms of cause and effect; most often they see them according to who's to blame. Young children feel they are to blame for a divorce even though blame was never even inferred by the parents. But without excessive reassurance to the contrary, it is inescapable that children will blame themselves, because their understanding is limited by immature intellectual brain development.

A six-year-old child once told me, "Maybe because I always get an ear infection, Daddy doesn't want to live here." Feeling they are at fault is their private secret, so they usually don't talk about it. They also don't talk about it because they don't believe they deserve to be comforted. After all, in their minds they are responsible for the bad situation. In my chambers I hear these private confessions. One child confided, "If I were to disappear, my parents would stop arguing and they both wouldn't be so sad."

It is difficult to convince children they are not to blame. This is why heroic parenting is essential. Heroic parenting involves going above and beyond the parenting you may be used to, despite your difficult relationship with your former spouse. I've come to believe that appropriate explanations about the divorce and why it happened need to be told and retold commensurate with the children's developing maturity. Most parents think that if they make the explanation in the beginning, then that hurdle is over. It is not. It is an ongoing process, perhaps into adulthood.

Risks of Mental Disorder and Anxiety

Dr. Judith Wallenstein reports in her long-term studies of children of divorced parents that fights over custody and visitation give rise to a greater incidence of mental disorders in such children.[1] They often do not fare well in school and have a greater incidence of suicide, attempted suicide, clinical depression, and other disorders.

Anxiety continues to be a theme in the children's lives well into adulthood. Dr. Wallenstein found that thirty years after divorce, many of them were still living with constant fear and were always waiting for disaster to strike without warning.[2] This anxiety takes away joy from their childhood, but it also takes away the ability to feel sustained happiness in adulthood.

After listening to hundreds of hours of psychological testimony about children and their parents, I have come to agree with Dr.
Wallenstein that the results of damage to children do not necessarily
show in childhood. They manifest themselves when the children are
adults and move into romantic relationships. These adults unwittingly
seek to duplicate their parents' marriage when they are creating their
own families. Not having a viable role model for relationships, they
often make bad choices or give up too soon, not having witnessed good
skills for dealing with adversity and conflict.

When Dr. Wallenstein interviewed children of divorce as adults,
she noted that they could not remember much about their childhood
playtime. They usually remembered worrying about arguments over
which parent was going to pick them up or where they were going to go
for the holidays. She found this troubling, because play is a vital part
of a child's social and moral development.[3] It is where children learn
about loyalty, conflict resolution, and generally fitting into the world
of their peers. Children who worry about their parents, their parents'
case, or taking care of their parents cannot be free from care. The
lightheartedness of youth is the place where creativity and a fantasy
life develop. It is the fantasy life that creates the optimism that tells us
that all things are possible.

Children as Caregivers

At the time of separation, one of the ways parents cope is by giving
children enhanced status. Sometimes parents say their children now
are the only thing that gives meaning to their life. Many children automatically move to fill the vacuum created by the parent who left and
attempt to take care of the remaining parent, who may be having a difficult time. Children tend to sympathize with the parent who wants the
marriage restored or respond to the distress of the aggrieved parent.
Caregiver children take on the responsibility of keeping the parent
going by acting in whatever role they need to play. That may include
being a confidant, surrogate spouse, adviser, or coach. In this way the

parent comes to rely heavily on the children in order to get his or her needs met. It gives the children a temporary sense of self-worth to be able to feel as though they're rescuing their parent. Parents who allow and encourage this are not really aware of the high price the children will pay later for being caretakers instead of children.

Ultimately, caregiving children may have a difficult time saying no to anybody in need, even when it is in their best interest to do so. As adults, these children are often unable to enjoy even the simplest things in life, because of their predilection to make sure everyone else is okay before *they* can be okay. They will give up everything—their joy, their fun, their ambition—to make sure everyone around them is taken care of. As adults, these children have a difficult time telling when things are their responsibility and when other people need to be responsible for themselves. In such situations emotional clarity is not available to them, so they are likely to take on more of the load in relationships.

In a case I had in my courtroom the wife, whose parents had divorced when she was a child, had lived with her depressed father. Even though she had come in for an order of protection, and restraining order, she now was unable to leave her abusive, alcoholic husband because "he needed her." She never felt she had permission to ask that her own needs be taken care of. She is just an example of children who grow up believing their needs will never be met, so they work hard to take care of someone else, hoping their mate will return the support. Even in the worst of times, these caregiving children find it difficult to accept comfort, because it feels alien.

In the wake of losing a spouse, there is a void where that spousal attachment used to be. Often parents understandably try to fill that void with exaggerated attention to their children. Children actually need more attention, more guidance, and more tenderness during this stressful time of transition. But when it is done to fulfill the parents' need rather than enhance the children's welfare—when parents fill their hollow space by using their children—it can be destructive. These parents may also fear losing control over their children, because they believe the legal process will somehow separate them from their children. It is as if their control of their children is the magic ingredient for their own success and safety. This kind of attention may make children feel they are responsible for eliminating their parents' sorrow. The consequences are staggering, because children cannot do that; they can only fail in their attempts, leading to guilt and feelings of inadequacy. To be responsible for parents' happiness and identity is too great a burden for children, whose spirit should be light, happy, and playful.

Creating Detrimental Defenses

Beth Erickson, in her book *Longing for Dad: Father Loss and Its Impact*, offers a useful way to think of defense mechanisms, which include mental processes such as denial, rationalization, and repression. She describes them as a physical talent. Children unconsciously grow a shield to protect themselves from the pain of being hurt again. This defensive pattern of shielding provides protection in childhood, but leaves emotional scars that can later create chaos in relationships.[4]

Erickson tells us that children develop these intricate defensive systems to keep their feelings suppressed, as it becomes intolerable for them to feel sadness or fear. Once the technique of suppressing emotions is fully integrated into a child's psyche, the emotional thermostat is not selective; good feelings get shut down as well as difficult ones. Therapy and other ways of working through problems actually become difficult later in life, because these children first have to admit to the feelings they have worked so hard to cover up.

Fear of Conflict

If children of divorce observe conflict being dealt with primarily by explosion, running away, or complete shutdown, they can develop a fear of conflict. They only remember conflict as the disastrous prelude to their parents' divorce, without the benefit of seeing difficulties worked through as they might in an intact marriage. When young children, who have not yet separated from their parents, hear their parents arguing, they believe they are part of the argument and therefore part of the problem. Imagine being sick, going into surgery, and hearing two of your doctors having a hostile argument over your case. When the people you're depending on behave this way, wouldn't you feel uncertain and insecure about your future? For the child of divorce, even the smallest conflict could signal a cataclysmic event.

As we all know, successful relationships are in large part dependent upon successful resolution of conflict. You may not have your needs met unless you are willing to ask for what you need—and fearlessly face the risk of conflict if the other person doesn't agree with you. If you can't ask for what you need, ultimately you may find the relationship unsatisfactory, even though you've never really given your mate a chance. The notion that working through conflict can make two people even closer and be a bonding event is an unknown concept for children of divorce. Adversity skills make up one of the greatest toolkits you can give your child. Reducing their fear of conflict and adversity will help them ask for what they need and say what they don't like, giving themselves a fighting chance to find and sustain happiness.

Dating and the New Love

Your children have just recently lost their primary family, the only family they have ever known. During this time of adjustment, they are seeking predictability and stability. If you expose them to a new person in your life too soon, they may not have the resources to adapt to yet another new situation. On the other hand, there is also the risk that children will attach prematurely to someone who may not be around for the long haul. Each of these new situations reactivates the insecurity of the initial loss of a parent. And when a series of relationships revolve in and out of children's lives, there is a cumulative impact, causing even greater harm.

When a new adult is brought into the family circle, the parent is necessarily preoccupied with him or her. The parental bond with the children that should be maintained and enhanced, especially during this difficult time, is watered down with the presence of a third party too soon. Even though arguments have been made that it is better for the children if the parent is in a good mood because of a new relationship, I don't always agree. I think it is important that the children feel they are a source of a parent's pleasure and that it does not take a new partner to make that parent feel good. When a new person comes on board too soon, it may appear to the children that that person is needed to make their parent happy.

I'm not suggesting that you should not ever begin a new relationship during a divorce. Just keep your children emotionally and psychologically protected until the relationship has entered a stable, secure stage. If your children are being very unreceptive and appear to be agitated or unhappy with your new relationship, they may still be in the yellow "caution" zone.

Daddy "So-Long" Legs

Children who are abandoned by one or more of their divorced parents may face significant problems not only as children, but also as adults. Abandoned children feel an overwhelming sense of rejection. Their thoughts are that the parents no longer love or want them or care what happens to them. These thoughts are potentially devastating to their self-esteem and ability to form healthy, loving relationships. The feeling that they are not good enough to keep a parent around physically or emotionally will impact them throughout life whenever the issue of self-worth erupts. Should they ask for a raise? Can they sustain lasting love? When will their friends or loved ones leave them? If they succeed, aren't they really just a fraud?

Children who are abandoned need to be reassured continually that they did nothing to cause the parent to leave, that the parent who left has his or her own problems, and that the children are very much loved and lovable. Most children who have experienced abandonment will greatly benefit from access to good gender role models of the parent who left.

As expected, abandoned children as adults often gear many of their actions to protecting themselves from the fear of being alone and replaying their childhood abandonment. I see these children get into difficult and abusive relationships, but have a difficult time leaving anyone who gives them attention, even if it is harmful. When these harmful relationships are over, I often hear these adults blaming themselves: "I shouldn't have asked him to call me more often," or, "Maybe I should have bought her a better present for Christmas." They have a proclivity for taking the blame when someone leaves them. Getting through to the abandoning parents on some days is the reason I am a judge.

Children's Complaints to Me

The main complaint I get when I interview children is that no one has explained the divorce to them, or when someone did, the reasons did not sound authentic. Platitudes were offered in an attempt to disguise what really happened, such as, "Mommy and Daddy have different goals in life." An explanation like this falls flat, because not many children know what goals are or why different ones would cause a breakup. If inauthentic or incomprehensible reasons are offered, children are even more baffled than if they get no explanation at all. Providing understandable reasons should not be confused with complete disclosure. Children should rarely be told anything that would harm them.

For the majority of children I have interviewed in my chambers, the most common emotion is anger. It is less so for younger children, because it is difficult for them to feel angry with a parent they are afraid of losing. With older children, anger comes out in ways that may seem unrelated to the person with whom they are angry. They may do poorly at school or fight with their peers. Some of the things children have told me they are angry about are:

Not being protected in the divorce process and being encouraged to choose sides

Being left by one or more parents

Feeling angry at themselves because they could not save their parents' marriage

Having to take care of their parents or siblings

Being a child from a "divorced family"

Court fights over visitation or custody

More than twenty-five years ago, I was appointed attorney for a four-year-old girl who was the subject of a heated, vicious custody battle that persisted for nearly eight years. Last year the child, now in her early thirties, called and asked permission to visit me so she could ask me a question. It was: "Why did my parents hate me so much that they put me through eight years of terror?" When I told her they fought over her because they loved her, she said, "Nobody who loves their child would put their child through that." As soon as she was old enough, she moved overseas to get away from both of them and rarely comes back. Was there a winner in that divorce?

At this point you may find that you are feeling quite emotional. I didn't write this to cause you grief or to make you feel guilty. I hope to inspire you emotionally or intellectually to take action to protect your children in ways you may not have done before or to feel good that you are doing many right things. If you are reading this, I know you love your children and may be angry with me for suggesting that you are not taking all measures to protect them. Not everything in this chapter applies to every child or parent, nor are the consequences always going to be the same, but the probabilities are too high to go unmentioned.

The next chapter, "Wisdom-Building Skills for Parents," offers expanded solutions and ideas to help your children. The children just want to go home, but they don't know where home is. Home is a feeling, not a place. Home is predictable, warm, and safe. Those things don't need bricks and mortar or bundles of money; they just need your heart.

11

Wisdom-Building Skills for Parents

The first step and maybe the most difficult is telling your children about your divorce. Following are suggestions to use when scripting what you are going to tell your children about your breakup. Ideally, both parents together will have this talk with their children. The children feel safer if it appears the parents are going to work together on the reinvention of their lives. This may be the most important discussion you will ever have with your children, so there is no such thing as too much preparation. These suggestions are appropriate for children of any age:

Mom and Dad have problems with each other and cannot live together. We have tried very hard to work out the problems and decided that living separately would be better. It has nothing to do with you; it is strictly between Mom and Dad. We are sorry that this is causing you pain, but we are going to work together to help take the pain away.

I know it feels very unfair that you should be affected by our problems. We very much wish that we could have worked them out. We are going to work together, so that the changes made in our family will work out for you. There is nothing we could've done to stop this; it is a grownup problem, created by grownups and solved by grownups.

We will not be living together anymore, and you will be having two homes instead of one. No matter where either of us lives, we will not love you any less, and we will always be your family. Mom and Dad are just going to live in separate houses.

We [or I] will always be available for you to ask questions and say absolutely anything on your mind. Sometimes people feel angry, sometimes they feel hurt, and sometimes they worry. All of this is okay.

If your children are young, they may not know how to ask questions, but they may want to. Try to anticipate what questions might be on their minds and ask them if those topics are things they are wondering about.

If the children don't respond, understand that they are going through their own process. You can say to them, "You may need to think about this a little bit. We can talk a little later if you want to."

You don't want to sound mysterious; you want to sound authentic. Preparation will help prevent and refine answers. Be clear and consistent in your delivery. If your breakup is shrouded in mystery, your children will think there is more bad news to come and that adults may not be telling the truth when they say things are going to be all right—under the surface danger may be lurking.

When both parents tell the children together, it minimizes the fear that they are going to be abandoned by one parent, and they will feel safer with the appearance of a cooperating unit. If there is too much animosity between the parents, however, one parent should tell the children as soon as possible so they can make sense of the parental conflict.

Be sure to have individual conversations with each child alone. A conversation with a six-year-old obviously is very different from one with a twelve-year-old. If the children are young, the talks will be shorter. If the children are older, let them talk for as long as they need to. If they want to terminate the conversation, assure them you are available at any time to continue.

Your children will immediately turn into little Geiger counters, trying to pick up evidence of changes in routine that will affect them. It is important to restore routines and family rituals as soon as possible. The more consistent home life is, the better.

It is best to help children with their homework and school projects and activities, even though you have less time and energy than you did before. They will be keeping a hard eye on you to see if you still have time for them. Can you still be interested in these small things that are very important to them? It is essential for them to know that if they need extra guidance, they will get it.

Preteens and Teens

Developmentally, preteens and teens are striving to figure out who they are. It matters how they look, what they wear, how they are accepted by their peers, what they are good at, and so forth. There are also physical and developmental changes. Their self-evaluation is endless. They want to be independent, yet they want the safety net of an intact family.

Usually teenagers do not blame themselves for a divorce to the extent that younger children do. But they grasp the concept of blame, and usually they blame at least one of the parents for the divorce. When they assess the meaning of their parents' divorce, they start to question their self-worth. It is troubling to them if they believe they come from parents who could not get their act together. If their parents couldn't get their act together, what does that say about their own chances? Often the anger teenagers experience is not directed against the parents, even when they blame them, but results in acting out, failing grades, depression, or lashing out at friends. If your child is a teenager, choose your battles carefully. Teenagers tend to be angrier than younger children and have an opinion about who is to blame. In essence, they may be looking for a fight.

Traversing the Truth

This section is designed to help you discover how you view the function of truth in relation to what you are going to tell your children about your divorce. Remember that your communications will not only consist of the words you say; in fact, your children will pay as much attention to your nonverbal cues. You may have questions during and after the divorce about how much of the truth they need to know. As those questions come up, your children will get a read from you even if you are evasive. You may also have challenging questions about how to sculpt the truth so it is not damaging to your children.

Following is an inventory to help you access your underlying beliefs about what you think is right to tell your children. For every truth you plan to tell your children, I suggest you first ask yourself how it might damage them. Regardless of how sophisticated your children may sound (thanks to the media and their access to the Internet), your children are not emotionally developed enough to know how to process harmful truths. Once you are clearer on your own underlying beliefs, you can protect your children not only from what you say, but what you don't say. Unspoken negativity can be just as potent. I have heard parents say, "I have never said a word against their father [or mother]." They don't have to; there are a thousand ways to transmit negative sentiments nonverbally. The movement of the eyes alone can convey more than one hundred separate and distinct emotions, opinions, and impressions.

Truth, although essential to the trust you create with your children, does not include topics that malign their other parent or in any way hurt the children. You might say to me: "My spouse cheated on me. Aren't my children supposed to know the truth? Are you asking me to lie to them, so I don't hurt them?" If I asked you to list twenty things your spouse has done wrong, you may be right about most of them. The key question is: Is being right, or being honest, when it may do harm, more important than your child's happiness?

Being willing to do this exercise—and it is difficult—is one of the finest examples of heroic parenting I know:

- Make a list of all the lies (even white lies) you have told your children about your breakup.
- Make a list of every time you exaggerated the bad behavior of your spouse to make yourself look better.
- Make a list of all your perceived truths that, if communicated to your children, might hurt them.

Are you willing to set aside some of the more damaging elements of the truth for now in order to protect your children in their vulnerable state? Learning damaging things about a parent is similar to the adult experience of being betrayed by a loved one or friend. It completely destabilizes your reality.

Suggestions for Communicating with Your Children

Don't give your children advice until they have completely said their piece and seem to feel understood.

Don't dismiss your children's complaints about what is happening in their lives with their friends, siblings, school, or other activities. These complaints may be indications of deeper problems. Even if they are small matters, your children need assurances that their problems are not going to be lost in the confusion.

Get to know your children's friends, so you can help your children have social encounters when they may not be feeling outgoing or may be depressed.

Give each child some private attention every day.

Don't criticize your children's emotions; they are very real. Don't tell them they should "get over" something.

Share with your children how you handled social difficulties when you were their age. Be honest about what you didn't handle well, and talk about how you see things differently now.

Do not criticize, malign, or in any way speak poorly of your spouse or former spouse.

Explain inappropriate reactions on your part. Unfortunately, it is not easy to hide bad moods from your children. Because many younger children consider a divorce their fault, it follows that they may consider your bad mood their fault as well. It is important to explain to them that your mood is not based on anything they have done. If they have done something and you overreact, explain to them that you may be overreacting because you are thinking about other things that don't have anything to do with them. For example, you might say: "I am not happy that you did not straighten your room like you promised, but in addition to that I had other things on my mind that had nothing to do with you at all." The trick is to separate appropriate parental emotions, like disappointment, from agitated emotions that are a result of your divorce. It might be helpful to explain to your children that there have been times before when you felt bad and you have always gotten over them. This is a teachable moment in which to show them that bad feelings come and go.

When your children are struggling with a situation, compliment them by telling them you know how difficult the situation is and how well they are handling it.

Free-Speech Zone

Inform your children that you are creating a "free-speech zone," which is a conversation with your children for one hour a week, the same time every week. Everything in their life has changed, so they are not sure what they can speak about, what is off limits or what is okay. In this "zone," your children have the opportunity and the right to say whatever is on their minds, without criticism or retaliation. At times it will be very hard as a parent not to feel defensive, but the purpose of this hour is to make your children feel safe so they can speak freely about their emotions and fears.

If you feel the need to defend yourself, ask them if they would like an explanation from you. When you do defend yourself, if they ask you to, don't tell them they are wrong—just tell them you see the situation differently. Let your child know that the full panorama of feelings is acceptable and can be worked through. This process can teach them that feelings are transitory and not a permanent part of them. Give them examples, such as, "Yesterday you were mad at Sophia, and today you are playing soccer together outside," or, "Last week you were mad at Rodney for not inviting you to the movies, yet this Saturday he is sleeping over." They are not wrong about how they feel, but they might have misperceptions that you can gently help them work through.

If these conversations end up being defensive or combative, you will have a hard time getting them to sit down for the next one without dread. It is important that you communicate that feelings are manageable and not overwhelming. Try putting up a blackboard or a chart in the kitchen or family room that lists the names of all the feelings and at the top the days of the week. If on Monday ten-year-old Tom is feeling angry, let him put a checkmark in the box that says "anger." If he wants to, he can write the topic he is angry about. If this is diligently followed, when it's time for the "free-speech zone," Tom can talk about what he put on the board. After all, one of the goals is to get the children to talk about their emotions, so you can help them navigate solutions. An equally important goal is to let them see that what they were angry about on Monday did not matter on Saturday. This can teach them the impermanence of emotions. Another advantage to this "feelings board" is that children feel that what is going on with them is important, even when you can't give them immediate attention.

The No-Negatives Challenge Game

For one day a week, abstain from talking negatively about anybody. I advise you not to make an appointment with your lawyer or therapist on that day. No matter how much you might want to say something on that day, write it down, leave it, and see how you feel about it the next day. Let your children know you are doing that, and invite them to join if they want. By this point in their lives they have experienced their fair share of parental negativity. For them to hear their parents are making a conscious effort to change teaches them that people can alter unskillful behavior.

Safety Phrases

Give your children permission to use safety phrases, such as, "Please don't talk to me about that information," "Let's drop that subject," "I don't want to hear it," or, any other phrase your children make up. Those phrases give them a respectful way to buffer your intentional or unintentional attack on their other parent. Just because you are the parent doesn't mean you can trespass on their heart without their having the right to build a gate.

Your Anger Affects Your Children

Do you know how your anger is affecting your children? Below are two ways to take an inventory:

- Make a list of things that trigger your anger and cause you to act harshly or short-tempered. Note how these cause you to act or react with your children. Concentrate on one per week, and see if you can modify your behavior.
- Ask your children, if old enough, to make a list of the things they observe that make you angry or short-tempered. Tell them you will not be angry about anything they write on the list. Tell them you are going to work on one of the things on their list per week.

Your Child Is Not Your Therapist

How tired and worn down do you become when you are worried? Do you convey your worries and concerns to your children as a way of lessening your own burden? When you do this, your children may take on all the feelings you are experiencing. After all, you are the captain of the ship—do you want to share with them your fears that the ship may be going down? Sharing your ongoing worries with your children may teach them chronic anxiety as a way of life. As an adult, you may no longer worry after a problem has been resolved, but children may suffer long-term anxiety about a subject you have gotten over, leaving imprints in the soft clay of their emotional terrain. Children should not function in the role of therapist, adult friend, or spouse; they are not there to meet needs that are rightly fulfilled by adults.

Building Your Children's Community of Support

Often children respond to anxiety and stress by regressing to behaviors they long ago outgrew. Do not criticize or let siblings ridicule them for this. This regression is a mechanism for coping with stress. But if it continues over an extended period, consider getting them professional help. The same is true if children are experiencing extended periods of anxiety, sadness, eating or sleeping disorders, reduced interaction with friends, problems in school, and persistent unusual behavior, including use of alcohol or drugs in teenagers.

If grandparents have not chosen sides in an obvious and apparent way, and if they understand your commitment to not maligning the other parent, they (together with other relatives) are an excellent source of emotional security. They may provide extra emotional reserves at the times you are feeling depleted. They also give a sense of family continuity.

Teachers and caregivers should be informed when parents are separating. Let them know who will be picking up the children from school and whom to call in case of emergency. If you let them know what's going on, they can give your child extra attention and can apprise you of any problematic changes in your child's behavior. Teachers are often the first to notice a child is under stress.

Many schools have psychologists and social workers to help children of divorce. Find out what resources are available. Social workers can help you get in touch with resources in your community. Most hospitals have sliding fee scales for children's therapy. Sometimes children feel quite lonely and could benefit from support groups, even if they are afraid to show their emotions. Even if your children appear to be okay, do not minimize their ability to shut down their own emotions in order to take care of yours.

Most people are wired to desire connection with other people. If a group does not already exist, create one at your church or in your living room for people to support each other in the never-ending struggle to take the high road during divorce (see Chapter 16, "Building a Practice Circle"). This group could emphasize protecting their children while helping each other navigate difficult situations. You might want to write your own group manifesto about how you want to treat your children during the divorce.

Introducing a New Relationship

After all the difficulties of breakup, you may welcome the positive addition of a new person in your life. Here are some suggestions to ensure that what may be positive for you isn't negative for your children:

Discuss with your children where you met the new person you are bringing home. This gives them context as they try to visualize where this person came from.

Tell your children how you feel about the new person. If the new person is only a friend, tell the children that too, so they don't worry about what he or she will mean in their lives if they don't have to.

If possible, discuss this new relationship with your former mate prior to making the introduction to your children. Don't forget—children worry that their other parent will be mad at them or hurt if they show affection or give attention to a new player. As discussed earlier in the chapter, children worry that one of their parents might lose interest in them, and they are afraid of doing anything that would risk a loss of love.

Give your children extra attention as a new relationship becomes more serious. Children of divorce often worry that they are going to lose the affection of their parent to the new person.

Avoid entering into a new relationship until your relationship with your former spouse has reached "heart money." Ideally, that is when the issues of money and emotions have come into relative balance. Until then, the household is trying to find its equilibrium, and surprising children with a new relationship can cause a foundation that hasn't even been built yet to tremor. The exceptions to this suggestion are those cases where money and emotions never come into balance, and it is not my intention to infer that you can never have a new relationship.

Traditions, Rituals, and Activities

Rituals restore or promote a sense of order and predictability. Restore old traditions, making them resemble their former structure as much as possible; they are signposts of stability for the family. Create new rituals as symbols of optimism for the newly configured family. Mealtime prayers are very comforting for young children and teenagers, while youngsters like bedtime prayers. The prayers do not have to be based on the teachings of any organized religion, but might include expressions of gratitude.

Encourage your children to become involved in a charity or get a family pet. Getting involved in altruistic activities distracts them from their sadness and teaches them at the same time to become compassionate toward others. If your family participates in organized religion, get your youngsters involved with the children's groups there. Spiritual centers are helpful in communicating a message of guidance during adversity and often support values other than material possessions. This may provide balance for the materialistic tendencies that children sometimes have during a divorce, because for the first time they might be noticing what they no longer have.

Encourage your children to have positive distractions from the family divorce difficulties. Hobbies, sports, vacations, and so on will get them out of the combat zone and enable their minds to focus on something else. If the money is available, and the children want to go, summer camp can be beneficial.

Helping Your Children Prepare for Visitation

The whole process of visitation is new for everybody. But the children are the ones moving back and forth, and in that sense they are the ones doing the "heavy lifting." Here are some suggestions to make the transitions easier.

The night before the visit, help them plan or let them do it by themselves, what they're going to wear and what they want to take with them, perhaps even what they want to do. In the beginning, stay liberal about whatever they choose to take. This process is unfamiliar to them, and they might think they need more of their things to help them feel more grounded.

Both parents should stick as close to the plan as possible. This is true both for the parent hosting the visitation and the parent who, sending the children off, may have made promises about what would happen during the visitation. Things might shift a little as time goes on, but in the beginning children are assessing what their lives are going to be like. Those lives were made unpredictable enough by the divorce; visitation should be as predictable as possible.

Don't discuss with your children the controversies you have with your spouse about parenting time; they will not understand the process of negotiating and compromise. When you do compromise, they may interpret this as your not fighting for them.

What Plays at Home Stays at Home

I recommend that you avoid questioning your children about what occurred during or how they felt about a visitation with the other parent. Often children are frightened that if they tell a parent they enjoyed their time with the other, the parent they are telling might love them less. Sometimes children feel they are betraying one parent if they feel they have to say something negative to appease the questioning parent. This question of loyalty should not require children to have to improvise how to handle parents on every, or any, visitation. Children should not be required to keep two sets of books.

You and your children should have guidelines about what can be discussed and what is private. For example, if your relationship with your former spouse is particularly harmonious, your innocent questions are not as detrimental, but for a while children will still have inner turmoil about the question of loyalty. Transfer of information between two households with the children as conduits is a recipe for disaster if there is conflict between the households. Potentially, either the children will manipulate the parents or the parents will manipulate the children.

Don't require your children to keep secrets from the other parent. Consider how difficult it is for you as an adult to keep a secret. Think about children who fear that if they cannot keep a secret, they may lose the parent's love. Secrets can easily become terrifying requests. Give your children permission to say, "I don't want to talk about what happened at Mommy's [or Daddy's] house."

How do you feel after reading about the damage to children that is caused by even the most loving parents? I would like you to write your feelings down, because although you are likely to feel strongly motivated to protect your children after reading this chapter, in the heat of the divorce process those protective feelings sometimes get overshadowed by what seem like greater concerns. Commemorate your feelings in writing, because the same mechanism that tells you your children are resilient will rise up to numb out those feelings you are having after reading this chapter. My hope is that, when you have to decide between numbing out or taking supportive action, you choose the latter.

I know this has been a heart-wrenching section to read, because I have revealed some difficult realities about how the divorcing process affects your children. I congratulate you for getting through it. Your children are lucky. But now I am going to reveal to you some other truths you need to know. The truth about the courtroom.

PART FOUR

TRANSFORMATIVE CONFRONTATION

12

Carnage in the Courtroom

It is easier to lead men to combat, stirring up their passion, than to restrain them and direct them toward the patient labors of peace.
—ANDRÉ GIDE

D o you swear to tell the truth, the whole truth, and nothing but the truth, so help you God?" This is always the first line heard as the curtain rises on the drama that portrays the dissolution of marital life. You quickly learn that this is not a polished Broadway play; it feels more like a bad home movie. You are sure this drama is about your life only because you have seen your name ominously written in black marker on large file boxes wheeled in by your soon-to-be ex's attorney. Oh, yes, you now call him or her "ex," instead of the father or mother of your children—this is the depersonalization necessary to go to battle. In those boxes is the "evidence against you." The venomous script reciting all your personal infractions that is coiled in those boxes, ready to strike, speaks volumes even before a word is uttered.

As you wait nervously for the judge to appear, the soundtrack from the movie *Jaws* plays in the back of your mind, and you surreptitiously study your attorney, hoping you have chosen wisely. Although you are sitting next to your attorney when the proceedings begin, it becomes clear that you are actually relegated to the backseat. It is a unique role you will soon be asked to play on the witness stand—a hero and a victim at the same time. Your spouse, with a parallel vision, is hoping to outplay you at the very same role.

That dual role may seem difficult, but not nearly as difficult as looking at your spouse and seeing in a single glance your former lover, now your adversary, standing behind enemy lines. The same hands that caressed you, that supported you when you were ill, are now vehemently shoving documents at an attorney in an attempt to administer pain instead of aid. You know those hands as well as you know your own, and for a moment it feels as though your own hands have turned against you. In this surreal moment that compresses love, hate, loyalty, and betrayal into one, it is almost impossible to find a rational center of gravity. This compression fatigue leaves you feeling dense, airless, and with a taste of metal in your mouth. You have penetrating needs to be met, but you are now not even sure what they are. You just know that, so far, the court system and the negotiating process have not given you any relief.

There is a culturally pervasive view that the willingness to engage in a court fight signifies strength or a show of resolve. My observation is that people often choose to let the courts resolve their differences when they need to feel powerful in a dispute. Often these people are unable to navigate through the emotion and pain of an argument with their spouse. It is much easier to scream, "See you in court, bitch!" than it is to negotiate through the myriad points of disagreement. In fact, the courageously mounted court fight may have nothing to do with the stated issue. In words of André Gide, "The most decisive actions of our life—I mean those that are most likely to decide the whole course of our future—are, more often than not, unconsidered."

If you have come as far as a court fight because your case could not be settled, you have already paid dearly. In order to lay down the tracks so that your locomotive can go full steam in court, you must have fully adopted a hostile attitude toward your spouse. With fear for your personal security amped up, there is a mutation of your otherwise peaceful and rational thought process. That mutation allows you to entertain such thoughts as, "Peaceful people can go to war," "Children can be insulated from this war; they are resilient and will get over it," and, "Because we haven't spoken in seven months, communication can never resume." Emotional short-circuits lead to fear-driven thought processes that provide a platform from which you can logically abandon all hope of fruitful negotiation.

There is no shortage of abusive behavior on court television to model. What you watch repeatedly can subconsciously stimulate an appetite for conflict that will be satiated only through anger and vengeance. Jerry Springer did for aggression in conflict what Carmen Miranda did for the banana. Too often litigants perform with high drama the roles and expectations for hostile behavior that seem approved of by popular culture. Television, one of the great formats for learning, has provided role models for the inhumane treatment of others. The people onscreen are not necessarily bad people; in fact, they are probably good people who have shut down their screening mechanisms and are behaving in ways they would not ordinarily behave. Creative solutions and positive ways of handling conflict have been drowned in a stagnant pool of resentments. When you decide the court system is your life raft, remember that this system creates electrifying tension and that the charge you get may be an emotional jolt you did not bank on.

Preparing for trial requires superhuman strength. Many people try to simultaneously mobilize sufficient reserves of the required negative emotion while trying to remain on moral high ground. An angry confrontation can alter the course of negotiations and with the flick of a switch lead a lost couple into a nasty divorce.

A woman involved in a divorce case came to my court for an order of protection. Her husband had spit on her in an argument in front of their children. She was outraged because of what the spitting had signified: anger, disrespect—even contempt. The husband admitted that he had spit. "But not at her," he claimed. "I was just so frustrated that I didn't know what else to say. I saw someone do that on Court TV." He could not access the appropriate language for his frustration; even his usual vocabulary of invectives came up short. Her interpretation of the spitting incident coupled with his inability to communicate his frustration had landed them in a bitter, albeit avoidable, court battle. What she really needed was a show of respect, and he needed to be heard.

Order in the Court Could Result in Disorder in Your Life

"How did you get here?" you ask yourself. "I had no choice. I had no options," you say. But it is not really as simple as that. When you find yourself at the end of your marital journey, it is excruciating to witness the brutality in the spouse you once loved, and to have a glimpse of your own brutal nature. You have shocked yourself with how easily, and even candidly, you revealed your spouse's personal secrets to your attorney and then published those private embarrassments in a public court record. There are rare exceptions, but in order to find yourself in court you have almost certainly had to align yourself with negative and often erroneous assumptions. Here are ten of the most misguided and, therefore, harmful convictions followed by some helpful truths.

Ten Detrimental Misconceptions About What Really Happens in Court

1. Destruction of your spouse is an acceptable means for getting what you need.

2. Your goals can be accomplished and sure victory attained by putting on a good fight. However, unlike traditional battle, where you can destroy and walk away, you might have to deal with your adversary for years to come.

3. Once you ignite a match in the courtroom, you can control the direction and intensity of the flames.

4. Your attorney will understand and execute your goals and desires in a way that satisfies your sensitivities and needs.

5. Your concept of fairness will approximate that of the judge's. You believe there is a clear-cut, nondiscretionary standard of justice that is not dependent upon the judge's personal values.

6. Your habitual negative thought patterns, fueled by well-developed propaganda to "create the enemy," will cease once the trial is over.

7. It is your spouse's fault you are at trial.

8. The judge wields a wand, not a gavel, and can magically solve your problems, no matter how much damage has been done to the family.

9. The court process will not hurt you, because you are invulnerable. In any case, whatever pain you feel will go away once the trial is over.

10. Your attorney can be vicious to your spouse, because that is your attorney's conduct, not yours. And people who are abusively cross-examined in court never hold it against their spouse.

Ten Truths to Dilute Some of Your Misconceptions

1. Winning is not necessarily a matter of being stronger or more effective, as it is in real battle, because the outcome is decided by a judge who will have only a snapshot of who you are or may not see your position the way you do.

2. You can rehearse your testimony until you have achieved perfection, but you have no way of knowing how you will be perceived on the witness stand. How well do you know yourself? Can you know how you will react when you are in an unfamiliar, pressure-cooker-type situation without any experience to guide you? I have seen the tightest cases fall apart when a testifier gets what I call "witness fever." Witness fever happens when the testifier has the irresistible urge to ad-lib testimony and discards the script.

3. The judge might ask an unexpected question that puts a stiletto directly into the soft spot of your case. Unexpected truths that you had never contemplated rise to the surface.

4. If you are going to trial on principle and are seeking to vindicate some moral standard that is crucial to you, you should know that moral standards and principles are not what courts are meant to address. Trials only address the law. For example, in a no-fault state, adultery is not relevant.

5. In your struggle for dominance over your spouse or the dominance of your legal position, you relinquish all control over your own familial and financial life. Ultimately you have no control over the outcome of your case. Unlike an architect, guided by a blueprint, a court battle is unpredictable. Court battles are unpredictable and laden with information that is not true and theories that do not hold up, while exhaustion and fear can color decisions you or your attorney must make in an instant.

6. Even in no-fault states, the courts are sensitive to helping victims and are sometimes punitive toward perpetrators of harm to a spouse or children. Attorneys know this. Attorneys might upgrade the decibels of the negative behavior or put a twisted spin on innocent behavior. A father had thrown the bat down after he struck out at a father-son Little League game; by the time the parties went to trial, the story turned into "the father tried to hit his son with the bat." The fruit of a hostile imagination about your spouse is at its ripest in court and takes the form of character assassination. Don't forget that your children may someday be able to get transcripts of the hearing.

7. Even under oath some people may lie. I have seen people lie about small things; one husband even lied about throwing out his wife's favorite shoes. Even the tiniest lie, once revealed, can completely ruin credibility. Many a well-rehearsed witness who is usually honest can be infected by the nervous dread of being caught in a small lie. The five hundred dollars you have in your sock drawer and didn't disclose, if revealed at trial, could destroy your case.

8. Ultimately you will have to take responsibility for your part of the hostilities you have set in motion in court. People love to come up to me at parties and tell me how the system ripped them off. By scapegoating we transfer some of our own responsibility onto the adversarial process. The court process is far from perfect, but not accepting your own responsibility will further entrench a victim mind-set.

9. Moving forward with your life is critical to the process of healing. A court battle requires freezing at the stage of blame and fault. The

debate escalates in court, focusing on who did what to whom. Character maligning becomes the focus rather than problem solving. This has an effect on you (and your relationship with your former spouse) that will last well beyond the end of the trial. Many people have told me years later that they wished they had never gone to trial because of how much it hurt them and their family.

10. The majority of cases that go to trial are not about the financial bottom line, but about an emotional attachment to a perceived righteous position. This attachment blocks the clarity that would allow a vision of the bigger picture.

Too often people end up in trial because they can't tolerate any more negotiations. You think you are at the end of your collective ability to problem-solve. But that is not true. You may not really be at a stalemate; you may just have stale negotiations. In this chapter I shared the truth about court battles as a motivator for settlement. As you will see, one of the great obstacles to settlement is expecting negotiation to be easy and come readily. In the next chapter I offer different ways to not give up.

13

Reinvigorating Stale Negotiations

On the one hand, there is the domineering pride of a victorious
conqueror. . . . On the other hand, there is a voice of reason
counseling against spending all one has, gambling away one's
last resource, in favor of retaining whatever is necessary for
an orderly retreat.
—CARL VON CLAUSEWITZ, *ON WAR*

Divorce negotiation, unlike other types of negotiation, happens
in a pressure cooker, at the last minute, and often in the halls
of the courthouse. Although the litigants might be quite familiar with the issues, their fear and anxiety centers are turned up
full blast. With emotional gut reactions often trumping thoughtful
problem-solving approaches, organized, direct modes of negotiation
often become derailed.

I noticed that when the parties or their lawyers became fatigued
and frustrated, they chose to relieve the frustration by going to trial.
It became clear to me that there were steps missing between reaching
the point of total frustration in negotiations and actually going to trial.
I believe this is where the phrase "from the frying pan into the fire"
must have come from, because that is what occurs at this juncture. I
developed the list below to give you a method for self-investigation, so
you can separate your emotions from the decision-making process and
identify unspoken issues and obstacles.

Everything on this list nudges rigid thought processes in a different way, but the goals are all the same: to use the cracks in the negotiation to shed new light instead of interpreting the cracks as flaws. It helps to remember that the road to settlement is not straight, but twisted and circuitous. These questions will help you travel that twisted but desirable road to resolution. In the divorce process the usual approach is "shoot first, ask questions later." When you use this list, you are asking questions first and only shooting as a last resort.

It is never too late to resume or instigate settlement negotiations. Very often cases settle after I say, "Call your first witness." Below is the list of questions to ask yourself prior to trial. You might want to bring this checklist with you to settlement negotiations or to court.

Checklist

1. Have you refused to continue negotiations out of pride or because you feel insulted or angry? Have you investigated the source of those feelings? Are there ways to deal with them that would allow the negotiations to continue?

2. Has your attorney explained mediation to you? Have you requested mediation? That request can be made any time prior to trial. This is beneficial at any point.

3. Have you done everything possible to reach a custody agreement? In pretrial custody negotiations, the parent with the weaker case usually gets more parenting time than he or she would at trial. At trial the judge uses a standard template and rarely customizes a parenting order the way a negotiated agreement would.

4. In financial negotiations, have you approximated the dollar amount that is in dispute that will result in a trial? For example, if you are $100,000 apart, have you calculated how much it will cost you and what you might lose at trial? Have you approximated spousal maintenance with no termination date? Paying both lawyers? Is there an objective person who can help you take the emotion out of these

calculations? Tell your attorney you want best-case, middle-range, and worst-case scenarios calculated.

5. Have you, alone or together, consulted someone who might offer emotional or spiritual guidance? This is beneficial at any point.

6. Do you know the ballpark figure for legal fees, including posttrial motions and costs like paralegals and court reporters? Ask your attorney to give you an estimate for trial.

7. Ask yourself if you are aligned with the principle that a negotiated settlement is better than a trial? Throwing the dice in court because you believe the judge will be sympathetic rarely results in doing better than negotiated offers or mediation.

8. Do you believe that accepting a compromise is a show of weakness? Do you feel bullied by your attorney into a settlement? Do you believe that settling is a "selling out of principles"? There is always a good basis for making compromises that don't appear to come from weakness. For example, compromises can be made for the sake of the family, proffered as a stroke of generosity, or stem from a realistic decision that "it's not worth fighting for."

9. Are you confident that your facts are accurate? Ask your attorney whether there are problems proving facts as you see them.

Pumping in Fresh Air: Taking Back Control of Your Case

The fumes of aggression travel back and forth in the courtroom, giving rise to a claustrophobic atmosphere that suffocates free and creative thought. Here are some suggestions for pumping fresh air into the proceedings to improve the possibilities for settlement, even after trial has begun.

Yes, negotiation can be tedious and frustrating, but that is a worthwhile price to pay to avoid a familial civil war. When I think about the difficulty of laborious negotiation that results in a well-drafted document that meets both parties' needs, I think of the words of Friedrich Nietzsche. He said "Fulfillment must come easily or not at all, a belief ruinous in its effect, for it leads us to withdraw prematurely from challenges that might have been overcome if only we had been prepared for the savagery legitimately demanded by almost everything valuable." In the end it is really a matter of comparative pain between two difficult processes and in that comparison, negotiation will always be the least painful.

- Whether you or your spouse is resisting settlement, reframe settlement offers in terms of their benefits to both parties, thus creating new roles of importance for both of you. For example, allow the dad to be the one in charge of homework, if that is of great emotional significance to him. Or agree to put the disputed money into a trust for the children, which allows everyone to be a hero.

- Don't be afraid to talk or communicate with your spouse if the opportunity presents itself, even in the courtroom or the halls outside. See if you can build an alliance to take back control from the judicial system. You both may be sufficiently frightened when you see what a trial is really like.

- When you have compromised, you know why you made concessions. When you leave it up to a judge, you may never know why certain decisions were made. I have seen people disconcerted for years, trying to figure out what happened at trial and why.

- Be open to all possibilities if overtures for settlement or even partial settlement are offered. Don't let the clamor of the battle leave you deaf to resolutions. Judges appreciate even small compromises and acts of reconciliation—even in the middle of battle—and will notice your attempts to make them. We keep a watchful eye on who is enjoying the fight and who is keeping the hostilities alive when they could be ended.

- It may feel as if you no longer know your spouse. Your spouse's thought process appears to have been ambushed by his or her attorney, family, and friends, especially that "new friend." You may feel opposition from sources you can't understand or predict. You must seek opportunities to bridge communications with your spouse.

- By the time you and your spouse reach the negotiation table, your demands will probably be fairly well solidified. It is helpful to consider the emotional component of your spouse's position. Some examples might be: the fear of paying money to a spouse may stem from the fear of being broke; a spouse's resistance to expanded visitation might stem from fear of losing the children. Understanding the fears of your spouse is not a basis for you to abandon self-protection. But if you understand the emotional component of your spouse's requests, you don't have to perceive those requests as insults or personal attacks. Feeling insulted and the resultant defensive posturing cause negotiation to break down.

- After a few negotiation sessions ask your attorney to circulate a draft agreement that can be subject to comments and criticism by both sides. Some couples I see cannot agree just because they can't conceptualize what an agreement would look like. It is simply too much to mentally organize without a schematic. On paper they can process it at their own pace on both the intellectual and the emotional level.

Obstacles to Negotiation

Shadowboxing

One of the single greatest reasons communications break down is what I call "shadowboxing." In shadowboxing, communication between the spouses breaks down, because they are no longer talking only to each other; one of the parties is still trying to negotiate based on the concerns of certain family members, who are not in the room but are controlling the case from the shadows. In my courtroom I refer to them as UFOs: unidentified family obstructionists. As long as communication with your spouse remains open, then at least you are negotiating one-on-one instead of potentially five-on-one. Recently in one of my cases the husband's father was completely controlling his financial decisions. Instead of leaving the father in the shadows where he could be as difficult as he wanted, I had him come to court. Only when he was actually part of the face-to-face negotiations could the case be settled.

Reactive Devaluation

Sometimes people react negatively to each other's proposals when they are influenced by a dynamic called "reactive devaluation." Essentially this means, "If it was my spouse's suggestion, I am suspicious." In court I am viewed as a more objective suggest-er. Attorneys might well frame suggestions for compromise as being jointly created. The goal here is the semblance of objectivity. A mediator or a trusted third party can do this as well.

Overzealous Attorney

You, not your attorney, will live with the life you create. If your attorney behaves in a way that is not in accord with how you want to remember yourself in the long run, it is your job to pull in the reins. Your attorney's job is to be an adversary, to be intimidating, to bully, and to appear to dominate the court. As time goes on you will find it more difficult to hide behind your attorney's behavior; you must impose accountability on yourself. You might benefit from the presence of a lower-key partner or mediator if there is an aggressive attorney involved who might have difficulty toning down the zealousness. A strong, perceptive, and intelligent attorney is very effective, but you don't want any personal conflict he or she may have with opposing counsel to be an added factor in your case.

Feeling Let Down by Your Attorney

Most attorneys dread that point when they have to urge a resistant client to consider settling the case. The timing is crucial, and when the

client is still simmering with righteous indignation over a real or perceived injustice, it will be hard for that client to listen to reason.

Ask your attorney to write down the benefits of compromising and
the risks of trial. If you are not ready to process these considerations,
no amount of logic and reasoned argument for a negotiated settlement
will be sufficient. When you feel your attorney is urging settlement
before you are ready, you may feel betrayed by your attorney, who you
perceive is "siding with the enemy." As your attorney explains to you
the reality of trial, you may also feel betrayed by the court system.

It is difficult to hear the realities of your case, including the pro-
clivities of the particular judge or jury, problems with the testimony of
a certain witness, or any of the other nuances in the law that could negatively affect the outcome. This is why you have to believe in the value
of negotiation. You have to be aligned with that principle to begin with.
Ask your attorney at the very beginning to keep you current with all
evolving realities of your case. This will prevent you from feeling bullied when you hear all the weaknesses in your case at the last minute.

Adding to Your Demands Once Concessions Are Made

The divorce negotiation process is packed with mistrust. One
way to exacerbate that mistrust is to keep adding on to your requests
every time your spouse approves one of your demands. If you keep
adding on, the other side will begin to believe that you see compromising as weakness and are simply using it as an opportunity to ask for
more. Try to ask for everything that you want in the beginning of the
negotiation.

Unwillingness to Admit a Mistake

Admission of error does not make you someone who is wrong, but
someone with a clear and analytical thought process. You can always
save face by deciding to put your family interests before a court fight.
You don't have to justify the mistakes. In fact, judges appreciate that
everyone makes mistakes in judgment; when that is admitted, you are

more credible across the board. Consider softening the process with an apology, an acknowledgment of misunderstanding, or some other symbolic gesture.

Not Acknowledging the Other Party's Efforts During the Marriage

Each party should acknowledge the other's contributions to the marriage, for example, parenting the children, providing financial security, or providing care during an illness. Litigants become frozen in their perspective and story line. If one side does not acknowledge efforts made during the marriage, the other side will often seek a trial so that the judge will tell the spouse how valuable the underappreciated one was. Judges note the propensity of the parties to ignore everything that went right in the marriage in favor of what went wrong. This tells judges something about the parties' perception, or, rather, lack of perception.

Defusing Frustration and the Breaking of Patience

Think about how frustrated you get waiting for airlines to book a flight or how fed up you get with your computer that you end up banging on the keys. Have you ever thrown something you were frustrated with and broken it? When you reach that level of frustration in negotiation, it's time to take a break. Then return to problem solving by listening and considering options instead of insisting on an immediate solution that goes your way. It is important to listen, process, then to work toward a solution. Do not accommodate an emotional urge to force an immediate solution.

Recognizing Exhaustion

Even if you are exhausted, do not relinquish your ability to negotiate. You may need a rest—take it. When you find yourself saying, "I give up, I give up," understand that you are exhausted. You can easily forget what you really need in your settlement when you are tired or nervous. A pressured or exhausted decision is not easy to live with, because you will always wonder if you would have decided differently if you were clear-headed and calm. Check to make sure your attorney is not becoming exhausted either.

If you are hungry, take a break and eat. When litigants are hungry, they become agitated and want to give up on negotiating just to get out of court. I can tell when attorneys get hungry, because they start disagreeing with what they have already agreed to.

The X Factor: The Hidden Obstacle to Settlement

You may believe you are the one who has done more of the compromising. You have reached the point where the negotiation zone has begun to feel uninhabitable, and the thought of giving up one more thing appears to be a show of weakness. Although at this point further negotiations are agonizing, the temporary torment is not as great as what you will experience at trial. When you notice that with all the compromising you have done there is still no settlement, there may be something you are missing that requires extra consideration. I call this the X Factor.

It is true that sometimes the only route to closure is a walk through the ring of fire: the trial. Surprisingly, this often doesn't happen because the parties cannot agree on a financial or custody settlement, but because one of the parties is not ready to terminate interaction with the spouse. This is the X Factor, or the hidden obstacle to settlement negotiations. I have seen this occur on countless occasions: the less-willing party is not ready to let go of the marital attachment. In these cases, even a negative and conflicted attachment appears preferable to no attachment at all.

After many years in the courtroom, I can immediately peg the combatants. I refer to them as the Initiator and the Resister. One is always more ready to move on, the Initiator; the other, the Resister, is still holding on. Sometimes the Resister catches up—sad but resigned. When that happens, the case reaches closure more quickly. Meanwhile, I observe with interest the body language, the word choices, and the way the estranged spouses look at each other on their first visit to the courtroom. If there is a great difference between the two levels of readiness for divorce, I mentally assign extra time to the case.

Timing and attitudes are always wild cards in the divorce process. These vary, depending upon whether the partners are in sync about the termination of their marriage or whether one is in denial that it is really over. It is important to understand these differences when negotiating. I have learned to avoid the error of believing that there is balanced commitment to ending a marriage. Differences in attitude affect the negotiations, and if not considered, they could result in an unnecessary trial.

Initiators often detach from the marriage earlier than the spouse. They have begun to concentrate on their new life. This is a bitter pill for the mate, who wonders if she has been asleep at the switch. Feeling powerless, she will now focus more on blame, fault, or what should have or could have been, obsessively wondering, "What did I do wrong?"

As the Initiator detaches, the Resister's role becomes smaller and smaller in the Initiator's life. This marginalization is often intensely painful for someone who is not ready to face the end of the marriage. So often, the case goes to trial primarily because this person wants to remain a factor, even a negative one, in the other person's life. This paradox is tragic to watch. The more vengeful and accusatory the Resister is, the more likely it is he or she does not want the divorce. What is sad and shocking about this is the Resister's ability to devote substantial amounts of time and money to the divorce process just to remain involved. Here's how it plays out.

As the Initiator's life appears to be moving toward a new future with a pleasant potential, an angry Resister can easily wipe the smile off the Initiator's face by forcing the focus to remain on the lawsuit, depositions, and documents instead of the prospective joys of the new life ahead. By saying, "I have moved on," the Initiator invites the Resister to use whatever remaining power he or she can summon to slow the Initiator's progress toward that "moving on." The Resister will do so even if it requires unreasonable negotiating, backing out on settlements, numerous attorneys, substantial attorneys' fees, or ulti-mately going to trial. "You will be happy when I say so" is the unspoken message.

The Initiator might suffer guilt for having broken up the family. This guilt is exacerbated when there is contact with the Resister and the Initiator has to absorb and witness the pain of the castoff spouse. Although many of us might believe guilt would make the Initiator kinder and more conciliatory, this is not always the case. Often the Initiator will avoid contact with the Resister to avoid guilt, resulting in a communication breakdown. Unfortunately, some guilt-ridden Initiators try to find ways to blame the Resister, making the Resister the "bad guy" to help alleviate feelings of guilt.

Among the most troubling and complex behaviors the Initiator may adopt is a twisted version of bait and switch. In this scenario, the Initiator is ready to move on, but for a variety of reasons leads the spouse to believe there is at least a chance of reconciliation. An Initiator who tries this disingenuous ploy can sometimes be trying to reduce the spouse's pain. Usually, however, this game is motivated by the Initiator's intense discomfort with being the one to leave the marriage. When this leads to optimism on the part of the hapless Resister, the Resister may fail to attend to the reparations and adaptations necessary for moving forward with life. The Resister may trade in her baggy jeans covering her extra fifty pounds, losing the fifty pounds and wearing spandex. Or she may have gone from couch potato to hot tomato in an effort to win back the Initiator's love. If it doesn't work, the Resister's pain increases because of the refreshed rejection, and the case becomes harder to settle. If the Initiator has connected romantically with a third party while creating the illusion of potential reconciliation, this can incite white-hot anger and feelings of betrayal in the Resister.

Even though Initiators are the ones who introduced the idea of divorce, they also go through emotional turmoil before reaching a decision. When they have finally made that decision, though, they can hardly wait to launch their new life, to settle into a new house, and to become involved in a new relationship, if they haven't already. Most of all, they are ready to rid themselves of their pain. When they fear their ship of happiness may not be able to leave the harbor, they grow impatient and agitated with the Resister. They perceive the Resister as anchoring them to the past, forcing them to relive it with blame and recrimination.

So often the Resister is taking that defiant stance out of fear of losing relevance in the Initiator's life. Mediation and counseling are especially good strategies for these types of cases. The parties must continue to deal with each other in a respectful way. Respective pain and fear are acknowledged rather than ignored. Neither party feels as if he or she is tossed away in a Hefty bag on the side of the highway, while the other one drives away in a red Corvette. If one party feels he or she is "easily walked away from," that party will surely find a way to make it not so easy.

The Last Act: Settlement or Battle?

As you look at your spouse standing in court, memories can flood your mind with sewage or sweetness. You can ruminate about your caravan of grievances or be grateful for what your mate added to your life. But to get through the trial, you must chloroform any good feelings you have for your spouse and deaden the part of the brain that holds fond memories.

By the time you go to trial, your hostility and resentment are so great it is impossible to thank your spouse for anything good he or she brought to your life. Because of this hostility, you have defined your years together by the snapshot of its ending. It is impossible to leave the courtroom and wish each other good luck as you both go off to begin your new lives. The court severs the bond with an ax; a settlement severs it with a handshake.

Using these principles of negotiation, in the next chapter we will go a step farther. You will see what a Civility Contract with your spouse looks like. If you and your spouse can communicate, you will find this very helpful. It is not for everybody, and its effectiveness varies depending upon emotions and readiness. Even if you say your spouse will never enter into this sort of contract in a million years, it is useful to know what it looks like, as you may want to build parts of it into your own proposals for settlement.

14

Your Civility Contract

We who lived in concentration camps can remember the men who
walked through the huts comforting others, giving away their
last piece of bread. They may have been few in number, but they
offer sufficient proof that everything can be taken from a man but
one thing: the last of human freedoms—to choose one's attitude
in any given set of circumstances, to choose one's own way.
—VIKTOR FRANKL, *MAN'S SEARCH FOR MEANING*

You now have the opportunity to write the final chapter of your
marriage on your own terms. The Civility Contract is a commitment by you and your spouse to design your divorce in a way
that respects and dignifies the time you spent together. A combative
divorce requires rightness or righteousness, whereas this endeavor
creates an atmosphere of protection and loyalty for you, your spouse,
and your children. The contract is an affirmation that the other parent,
your former spouse, is one of the most important people who were
ever in your life. Your children will know you value that relationship
and will continue to do so. Creating the contract is a tangible act that
merges the concepts of making amends, emotional healing, including
the enhancement of self-worth, and compassion.

The Personal Manifesto is an agreement you make with yourself.
The Civility Contract is an agreement you make with the person you
are divorcing. This chapter is for:

Those who want to address their divorce with the intention of co-operating.

Those who are confident that their spouse will not participate, but want to include some of the suggestions in this chapter in their final divorce agreements.

Those who are confident that their spouse will not participate, but want to enhance their ability to get their needs met through skilled communication.

Those couples who have not cooperated thus far, but now want a new way to complete their divorce.

Those who want a new way to interact with their former spouse after the divorce.

Those with children, who may use this chapter as the beginning of their dedication to heroic parenting and loyalty to the family they created.

Those who are already divorced and want to have better interaction with their former spouse.

Those who don't really care about communicating with their former spouse, but who realize, because the children are not thriving postdivorce, that they have to do something different.

Those who want a format for reconciliation.

If you are fully aware of all the emotionally challenging things that can arise in a divorce, you can prepare yourself in advance. If you agree with your spouse about a strategy to manage those challenging emotions, then spontaneous reactions may not result in the breakdown in communication and trust. Awareness of what to expect could be enough to make you hold your tongues when your impulse is to react with spite or anger. Although you can't predict the future, you can make a contract for damage control and influence what that future will be—alone or with your spouse.

A Remedy for Guilt

Few divorces leave the participants without some nagging remorse about what could have been done to prevent it. As we scan our behavior, we may decide that we were saints, but this is rare. If we hurt someone we once loved or our family, it may feel like a violation of our core values, which can give rise to shame and guilt. Guilt serves as an obstacle to keep us from moving out of pain, because it traps us in our melodrama about how much we have hurt someone else. Extended guilt is destructive, because it erodes self-worth. To maintain self-worth, we often engage in either denial and withdrawal or an immense amount of overcompensation directed at the people we think we have wronged. Because of the elusive quality of guilt, we do too much or too little to try to reduce it; it has an insatiable appetite, and it is hard to gauge the right amount to feed it.

Some of us take the path of withdrawal, because our spouse knows our secret crimes and unflattering qualities, and we want to distance ourselves from that harsh judgment. When we feel guilty, we frequently find ways to make ourselves suffer, or we try to reduce the power of the one we have wronged so that person doesn't have control over us. We don't want to be reminded of what we have done or not done, and in our spouse's face we see the etching of our sins. Emotionally, we don't feel safe unless our spouse is out of our line of vision or we are emotionally buying him or her off, a debt that has no final payment. Guilt replaces tenderness the same way a confession lamp replaces moonbeams.

Guilt has benefit if it calls us to account, but being "eaten up" by it is destructive. I have heard it said that good guilt lasts ten minutes and results in a behavioral change. If we have behaved poorly and recognize it, we can be motivated to do something differently. Once we come to that recognition, the person who did the original harmful behavior no longer exists. What exists now is a person who wants to change something. If we were to remain the same person, we would continue to do the same thing over and over without thinking about it. A way to make up injuries to our spouse and even our children is by committing ourselves to a behavioral protocol. One of the most potent sentences I know is, "I am sorry I have hurt you. Is there anything I can do to make this up to you?"

If you are considering creating a Civility Contract, you have developed an intention to make up to all concerned. Because this contract manages much free-floating guilt, your children can be spared having to pick up the loose debris of parental guilt and blame themselves. Guilt keeps you attached to unfinished business. By sticking around to finish business, you will have found a way to detach with honor while reducing guilt.

A couple came to my court to renegotiate a child-support agreement. The problem was that the husband, Dennis, an investment banker, wanted to pursue his lifelong dream of teaching. He had come to hate his job and was miserable, but at the same time he felt very guilty about his desire to teach. His wife, Lonnie, was furious, because she believed that he should not be allowed to "put his dream ahead of the needs of his children." To their credit they always communicated. At a pretrial conference I could see they were both concerned they would lose their satisfying working relationship as parents. I asked them whether it was possible to see this as a joint problem instead of an insult to Lonnie and the children. Lonnie was doubtful, but she had a lot at stake. She didn't want to become one of those people who "hated their ex."

The interesting aspect of this case was that in a sense everyone's needs were legitimate. It took months of negotiation, but they committed to no name-calling, not inferring negative motives on the part of the other person, and not criticizing each other. Without the blaming invective, an entirely different light was cast on the situation. Instead of making the situation worse, they became allies. The parties agreed that Dennis would try teaching for a year to see if the dream would turn out as he hoped. Dennis sold his car and put the money in escrow for the shortfall on his child support. Lonnie agreed that the child support could be somewhat lower if her former mother-in-law, Doris, helped with childcare. Doris committed to three days a week. This is an outcome that could have never happened if there had been an antagonistic hearing.

Reconnecting to Detach?

In a perfect world, people who witnessed you behaving badly would disappear, never again to remind you of your irrational anger when you threw that book, screamed with a voice you did not recognize, or revealed private confidences about your spouse to your friends. After some of your less-proud moments, it does take courage and bravery to be willing to communicate and reconnect with your spouse on a new level. As you begin your Civility Contract, you will notice that this protocol for separating has its own brand of intimacy. Your spouse knows you about as well as anyone can. By the time you reach the end of your marriage, your spouse will have seen you make many, many mistakes. What's worse, that behavior has been witnessed by somebody you may now view as an opponent. But in this contract you have chosen the one with your secrets and the one who could hurt you the most as your ally. It is a spiritual version of the political advice to "keep your friends close, your enemies closer." Reconnecting to create and adhere to the Civility Contract can feel intimate, but you have chosen to be intimate in a productive, life-enhancing way.

Suggestions for Your Civility Contract

The Civility Contract can be used for all communication or negotiation. You can create your own terms or modify any of the suggestions below. You will probably want to update them as time goes along. I think it is beneficial to make the original contract in writing, but written modifications to it may become cumbersome. Just make sure you both understand what you are agreeing to. The terms don't have to be written on a stone tablet—sometimes they will be on a napkin. Grammar doesn't count, and you don't need an English teacher to clean it up.

Keep in mind that some of the pain of breakup will exist no matter what the other party's behavior is like. Therefore, at times when you are in pain, it's not necessarily because the other person has done something wrong.

1. *Agree not to assume each other's motivations.* I have learned more as a judge through mistakes and false assumptions I have made than I have from the wisdom and knowledge of law books. Believing or acting upon assumptions about what other people are thinking or what their motivations might be is one certain way to destroy communication. No matter how well you might know them, you can never be sure what they are thinking, and you might be connecting them to a behavior they are trying to change.

2. *Agree to swiftly acknowledge errors and mistakes you have made.* If you yelled or snapped, violated this agreement, or did something you wished you hadn't, acknowledge it as soon as possible. The longer you wait to clear the air, the more time you and your spouse have to dwell, stew, and generally become angrier. As you build resentment, you will be less focused on moving forward to get out of pain. (See Chapter 8, "Apologies: Managing the Ebb and Flow of Trust.") If one party continues to break a certain promise, see if it can be revised in a way that is agreeable.

3. *Agree to accept that things will be said to one another that would have been better not said.* Sometimes people say inappropriate or unkind things because they are venting and cannot help themselves; other times they deliberately say things to hurt or make another angry, but it was the best they could do at the time. Know that this will happen and give each other space, as you both are under tremendous stress and weighed down by the continuing undercurrent of sadness that drains the energy required to be your best self.

4. *Practice patience with each other. Give each other permission to get frustrated and even angry.* Accomplishing just some of the goals of this agreement counts as success; don't expect continual triumphs. It may appear to you that your spouse is not modifying his or her behavior fast enough. Remember this is your spouse's path; there may be more issues for your spouse to work out than you think. It only means your spouse is continuing to suffer. Everyone learns in his or her own time.

5. *Tell your spouse when something is really bothering you, and resist letting it fester until the point of resentment.* If you don't tell each other when something is bothering you, then you aren't giving the other person the opportunity to correct the behavior. Ask about a good time to have this conversation, so the other will be receptive. Expect some defensiveness in the course of this process, but without communicating, it is harder to reduce your frustration with the other person.

6. *Agree that if you have an argument, you will not speak for a day unless you have figured out how to resolve the problem.* Unless you have a new way of addressing the problem or a new solution, rehashing without giving yourself time to get insight is not productive. The best way to do this is to write down the exact nature of your frustrations (just for yourself, not to send) rather than spontaneously sounding off to the other person. Spontaneity can be a wonderful thing in romance, but when you are going through a divorce and struggling to control your anger, it can usher in disaster. With spontaneity we can fling ourselves into the very pain we are trying to escape.

7. *Communicate with each other only until you reach that "no turning back" level of frustration.* Terminate such a session even if just one person is frustrated and the other wants to continue. Otherwise you risk sliding into the realm of animosity. When this happens, tell each other that it's okay and you will resume the discussion at a later date. Set a date that is mutually convenient. It's like putting up a white flag in battle. It's fine to say, "That's all I can do for today. I'm starting to get into some bad emotions." The goal is to build a new house, not burn it down with a few harsh words that ignite the flames.

8. *Agree that each of you can call for a "redo" of a conversation.* If you have had some insight and now know how to do something differently, ask if you can discuss an issue that went badly before. And don't punish the other person by withholding permission if they ask for a "redo" of a conversation.

9. *Reduce your requests for admissions of fault and give up the chicken-and-egg debate.* Try to give up the need for a steady diet of your spouse's

acknowledgment of the suffering he or she has caused you. Do not depend on this acknowledgment of fault to give you back your personal power. That must be self-generated. The more you turn inward for your sense of self-worth, the more you can fortify your strength. Who started the downward cycle is irrelevant, as the cycle requires an actor and a reactor.

10. *After you have an argument, agree to come up with two solutions to the problem before your discussion about who is to blame for starting the argument.* Blaming someone is an effort to reduce guilt or anxiety. People don't usually feel guilty when they believe their behavior is justified, but people are inclined to find justifications for the behavior to avoid guilt. If you agree to put solutions first, the blame discussion will become less interesting.

11. *Fake it till you make it.* Use all the self-discipline you can rally to behave compassionately until your real attitude catches up to your faux behavior. It will in time become more authentic, because you generate more peace for yourself when your choices are less destructive. You will gravitate to these choices as you discover how much better they make you feel. Perhaps you will "fake it" for your children, to make them feel safer. You and your spouse may agree to tell your children that Mommy and Daddy have worked out a contract together to protect them despite your differences.

12. *Every week give each other a new compliment. Reminisce once a week.* This is an exercise in resurrection. What can be brought back to life from the marriage that enlivens your life going forward? I am not talking about love or even liking, just good feelings from the past. At those times when you feel wronged, remind yourself of all the ways you benefited during your time together, whether it involves finances, career, building a family, or personal growth. Keeping a promise enhances trust, so as one of your compliments you might state your appreciation when your spouse keeps a promise.

Is It Too Late to Re-create?

You may be in the middle of a difficult divorce, or your divorce or separation might be years behind you. It is never too late to decide that
whatever you have done before has not served you or your family. If you
long for a new beginning, you may wonder if too much damage has been
done. You can continue to do more damage or try to bridge your way
back to civility. You don't have to love or even like your former spouse;
you just have to know you don't want to continue going on as you have.
In a recent case of mine, parents who had been divorced for ten years
and never spoke except in court finally had to find a way to make an alliance when their teenage daughter became pregnant. Her mother had
always maintained her daughter was doing just fine without her father,
but the daughter's psyche knew different. Currently the daughter and
the new baby are living with the daughter's father.

Yes, there will be emotional flashbacks. Trust will come slowly and
core resentments will be replayed in your mind for the hundredth time.
Begin by giving your former spouse a copy of this chapter and Chapter 7, "Forgiveness: Weapon of Mass Construction." I suggest you both
do the exercises in that chapter and share some of the results with each
other. If you have children, give your former spouse a copy of Chapter 9,
"Damage to Children: Developing the Heroic in Your Parenting." This
is a personal process, so if you are used to communicating only through
lawyers, you will have to become reacquainted with each other. Perhaps
you will notice that your former spouse has taken some responsibility
and has gained some insight into his or her previous unskilled behavior, or maybe old patterns will remind you of why you divorced in the
first place. Try not to expect or predict that your former spouse will keep
repeating old behavior; allow room for change. A therapist, mediator, or
other spiritual advisor can help you create your Civility Contract if you
need additional assistance.

A Four-Step Formula for Disagreement

Here are four suggestions to be used in any of your communications, with or without a Civility Contract:

1. *Validate the other person's perspective:* "I can understand why you want Jennifer on Wednesday. Your solution makes sense from your point of view."

2. *Give a reason you don't agree:* "I work all day, and Wednesday is the only day I get home early."

3. *Offer at least one alternative:* "What about every other Thursday?"

4. *Express your commitment to working out a solution:* "If we don't work it out today, I am sure we will find a solution in the near future."

Communication Protectors

Here are several suggestions for keeping communication on track:

1. Criticize the behavior, not the person. For example, you could say, "When you are late it drives me crazy, because the children can't finish homework, and I worry." Do not add, "You are selfish and don't care; you only care about yourself." Don't call the other names or offend.

2. Don't bring the past into your current expression of displeasure.

3. Don't say "always," "never," "I can remember the last time you . . . ," or "I know exactly how you operate."

4. Don't assume you know the other person's thoughts or motivation.

5. Let the other person have his or her say. Then when you think the other person is done, ask if that is so or if there is anything else he or she wants to add before you speak.

6. Don't terminate a conversation that is not going well by using phrases such as, "That's it," "I can't talk to you," or "You never listen." Instead, you can say, "I am too angry to talk now."

7. Don't escalate the problem by bringing in third parties who agree with you: "I told Martin what you did, and he thinks you are wrong and a jerk."

8. Stay on the subject you are talking about even if the other person gets onto another one. Say that the other subject is important, and you are willing to discuss it another time: "Right now I want to discuss Monday's visitation. We can talk about insurance after this topic is resolved."

Managing Your Expectations

Unrealistic expectations can undo much good, nobody can maintain perfect conduct. If you're on a diet and you slip up with a slice of cake, that doesn't mean you give up and polish off the rest of it. One unskilled action does not have to contaminate the whole day. If anything, the occasional failure could motivate you to try harder.

Remember, you are building a new entity here, so the agenda is different than when you were committed to your marriage or trying to save it. If you look at this process as an effort to build something new, perhaps this will help you be less sensitive to the sting of old resentments. You don't have to hold on to old resentments you had in the intact married relationship. This is a whole "New Deal."

On exceptional occasions I have seen couples in my courtroom on the final day of their marriage—knowing that it will end with a pronouncement that will change their lives—holding hands or rubbing each other's shoulders in comfort. These are people who understand that they are going through emotional surgery. Each is offering consolation and reassurance to the other. They hold on to one another for ballast as their respective boats leave the harbor into uncharted territory. They know there is no greater source of comfort than each other, and with generosity they offer it.

PART FIVE

EMBRACING THE ROAD AHEAD

15

Karma and the Recycling of Human Relationships

As a judge in family court, my daily hope is that divorce becomes less common. But the facts do not support my desire, and the cultural reality is that the national wedding bouquet is soon to be constructed of short-blooming day lilies. If this cultural fact were an ancient one, none of us would need this book. We would be conditioned to expect marital failure and would have the skills hard-wired in us to adapt to this predictable change. In the fight for personal survival, human beings must forever adapt to change. Each change, whether personal or environmental (change in the family, the house, the school, etc.), has potent accompanying emotions, and these emotions are the accelerators we use to build our ever-evolving future, positive or negative.

Unfortunately, multiple romantic relationships and the termination of those relationships have become part of our cultural evolution. For years I had hoped that that trend would be reversed, but we have been unable to escape this current reality. Nothing short of being locked in a cage with your mate, perhaps in a laboratory or a zoo, can immunize you completely from this cultural virus.

What Meaning Can We Find in Relationships That Did Not Last?

Since we have not yet found a cure for this epidemic, we must create a way to not only survive, but thrive in this reality. Marriage, an institution that had always provided a protective coating that supported the survival of the family, has thinned like the ozone layer. Never before have families been exposed to such challenges to sustainability. In our world, where we pride ourselves on innovative disposability and always trading up for the latest model, have we come to think of people and what they have brought to our lives as discardable as well? Even though we all want to be on the positive side of the 50 percent divorce statistics, our reality has been expanded to include acceptance that relationships may not be built to last.

The question then, is: what meaning can we find in relationships that did not last? We must find a different way to look at those people who we previously loved. Sprayed with a mist of obsolescence, our loved ones appear to have diminished value. Because of the impermanence of relationships, many find it unwise to allow themselves to be really vulnerable with others. When we are guarding our vulnerability, it becomes more difficult to attach, but it is vulnerability that promotes attachment.

Ultimately, there may be a part of ourselves that we hold back in a relationship. I am always asked why I think the divorce rate is so high. Perhaps this holding back is not only a reason for the increase in antagonistic divorces, but also one of the reasons for the lack of sustainability of marriages. Without the mortar of intrinsic worth, many of today's marriages seem to be built out of Lego blocks that may be snapped together or pulled apart at will.

Believing that our mate's value lies only in his or her present functionality to us, we measure people's worth only in terms of current value. How, then, do we treasure our time on earth if relationships are only fragmented and episodic, and have not been woven into the big picture of our lives? In a world of replaceability, we have begun stripping away a whole layer of human-relationship value that gives our life meaning and spiritual connectedness. The platinum emotion of love can turn into tomorrow's waste material. We are all in peril of being looked at with the glint of expendability in our beloved's eye. With this mind-set, how can we value loyalty and devotion to the family unit or to anyone? With the increasing number of multiple broken relationships, we have all accumulated a landfill of human memories that can be either relegated to waste or productively recycled. The only way to redeem this landfill is to upgrade the value of its contents from toxic to timeless.

Suffering is the by-product of the divorce epidemic, so the search is not only for how to live and weather the turmoil, but how to make sense of it. Friedrich Nietzsche wrote, "What really makes one indignant about suffering isn't the thing itself, but the senselessness of it." As with many difficult life experiences we ask ourselves, what purpose does this serve? In the end, the question is: Does this suffering motivate us to want to change our lives to reflect our ultimate purpose? Has this suffering inspired us to ask questions about the meaning of our lives?

As long as we see our suffering as senseless, it is eviscerating. The Good Karma Divorce way of using suffering will always be applicable, no matter what the crisis. If we were continually in a state of bliss, we would never seek answers to questions about the meaning of life, because we would not want to tip the delicate balance of that state of well-being. We would always shield ourselves from being penetrated with life-altering questions. My view of pain is that it is meant to keep the blood of wisdom circulating. After reading *The Good Karma Divorce*, it is hoped you have assembled much wisdom. You now have the opportunity to live that wisdom. Learning from love and the pain of the disintegration of that love is a valuable use of our time alive.

It is never easy being true to the person we want to be or staying true to our values. There is no place of respite. As soon as we are comfortable with a new ordering of our reality, it changes. During our divorce we try desperately to control our spouse, the system, and our experiences. If we had that much control, we would never choose to be in any pain. But we are not supposed to have that much control. The better path is to stay open to all of life's experiences—that is what liberation is all about. That is freedom. If you think you have figured out the ending of your current crisis or anything else that happens in your life, then your projection probably wasn't "great" enough. You may have limited your possibilities by trying to control or mold what you think would happen, positively or negatively. You may have limited your vision and cut off the chance for spectacular possibilities.

The process of the Good Karma Divorce can be adapted to all human struggles, as it is based on the knowledge that the purpose of pain is transformation. We don't hide from it. We use it, as soon as possible. When we are less resistant to the changes of life, we will be more adaptable. When we don't fear change, we can be sensitive to nuances and so many things we would have otherwise missed, the main ones being clues about those spectacular possibilities and the attainment of our life's purpose.

Back to the Future: Memories

Even though we are detaching from our mate, I have given much value to the handling of our memories. Marriage creates an expansive field of memories, effervescently rich with the potential to fertilize our new life. Keeping alive good recollections ensures that our arteries will carry those memories to our heart, so that our heart will not be deprived of nourishment from our past. We know that love can die when we forget to nourish the source; we have made that mistake before. Now we know that if we replenish the value of our past, it may feed us in the present. History is foundational. Our choice is to tell ourselves that our marital history was always depleted, or that there were, at least for a time, the creation of valuable nutrients we can still use. It is this enhanced respect for our past that makes the path suggested in *The Good Karma Divorce* easier to follow.

Memory is not only part of the past, it is alive in us now. If its interpretation is negative, it has the potential for self-laceration. Your history with your former spouse is a joint project. You cannot annihilate these memories without also killing off meaningful parts of yourself. You must do something with these memories, as they remain in your bloodstream. When you accept that you have deposited parts of yourself in his or her soul, you can comfortably retrieve all the richness of your experiences, pain as well as joy.

We all have created rooms where our past selves are stored. Do you want that storeroom to be dark, damp, and without air or usable and full of wisdom? This book is about recovering something and finding something. It is about recovering the person we know ourselves to be and finding a path for that person to travel on. The memories will have to be stored somewhere; the trick is to not store them in oblivion. If you believe that in order to move through the door ahead, the door behind you must be sealed, you may be entering the gates of prison.

Good Karma Divorce: Put Your Brain on a New Diet

Because there is no resting place in life, we will always have an opportunity to change and evolve. Even if only a portion of *The Good Karma Divorce* resonated for you, an unexpected magic door will still open for you.

Until recently it was believed that, after childhood, the brain was fairly permanent. The only changes that took place happened when the brain started to decline because of old age. Science now tells us that the brain has neuroplasticity: it can change and alter its structure, become more agile, vital, and vibrant at any time until we die. Dr. Norman Doidge, author of *The Brain That Changes Itself,* tells us that this occurs through novelty, new habits, hobbies, or different ways of responding and thinking.[1] As a matter of fact, this is the diet the brain craves.

The Good Karma Divorce puts your neuropathways on a new diet. After following only some of the suggestions and exercises offered in this book, you will have altered some perceptions and changed behaviors and thoughts in novel ways. Because these alterations are new, you will have increased your brain's energy, agility, intensity, and rejuvenative abilities. The wonder is that in the trenches of adversity, and disguised as devastation, we have come across the magic door. As Peter Coyote says in narrating the PBS TV show *The Brain Fitness Program,* "You will be able to live your life till its end . . . full of it."

Divorce as an Avatar of Karma

Living is a constant birth process rather than a wearing-out process.
—Chogyam Trungpa

Many people mistakenly consider karma and fate to be the same thing. Fate is the concept that the path of one's life is predetermined. Karma, on the other hand, connotes the ability to alter one's life by altering one's thoughts and actions. You could say karma is a way to make your own fate. In this book the concept of karma helps us understand a process of personal transformation, a living rebirth, brought about now by good thoughts and actions. We do not have to wait until the next life to notice the effects.

Suffering is considered an opportunity to refine our behavior and in so doing purify our karma. You are going through a divorce, and your chance has arrived to change your perceptions—and perhaps limited views—of happiness. Yes, your spouse has unwittingly gifted you all of this. Your spouse has helped you see pain in a different way. Divorce hits us on every level of existence. You didn't want divorce to happen, but because it has, it is the perfect vehicle for personal transformation. Divorce is just the emissary delivering your opportunity to you. In your struggle to enhance your karma or just to become liberated from your pain, you have found a way to work with any crisis. You don't need to be concerned about obtaining good karma at some future time, as rewards happen for you in the very moment you take a different path to healing.

Look at the Good Karma Divorce as a way to clean the house where you are going to live in the future and a way to keep you from dumping waste into your next relationship. Your house no longer has dark shadows, closets stuffed with anger, or drawers holding remorse. You have laid bare and then altered the harmful aspects of divorce while working to protect your family's emotional DNA for generations to come. As you move into the next chapter of your life, you no longer have to stay on guard. You are now ready to be captured by the karmic cameras.

16

Building a Practice Circle

Profound and collective dread permeates the very idea of divorce, drawing from decades of scorched-earth horror stories of the damage wrought when spouses declare war upon each other. But those who embark upon the divorce journey have choices. Will they accept the conventional wisdom that in divorce it is acceptable, if not unavoidable, to abandon civility, fairness, and compassion for an all's-fair-in-love-and-war approach? Or will they endure the risks with grace, strength, and integrity in order to make the passage to a better place? Will they conquer their justified fear of the unknown, because they see on the horizon the potential for their own heroic voyage to a new world of growth and self-understanding?

When an inadequate but entrenched belief system is successfully challenged, there are periods of resistance, transition, and, finally, acceptance. I believe that divorce in our society has reached a tipping point. One might have thought that by now we would be rather used to a society of fractured families. However, the increasing frequency of divorce has not accustomed us to the pain; rather, it has increased our collective dread.

To voyage successfully to new worlds of personal enlightenment and expansion in the face of a culture that supports a warring mentality for divorce, we must learn to navigate according to different stars. We will need a trustworthy and committed crew to help us along the way. To accomplish this I suggest the Practice Circle—a small group of individuals committed to exploring and applying the principles and strategies found in *The Good Karma Divorce* together.

Pain shared is pain diluted. Life's difficult passages are best navigated in the company of like-minded travelers. Too often, however, I see divorcing couples caught up in a vortex of negative and thoroughly un-productive feedback from friends, relatives, and even attorneys. Many people have limited support, because their families live in different states or their contact with married friends and in-laws has diminished. The Practice Circle is a way to create a communal experience.

By design, the Practice Circle is an all-volunteer effort. Entry into it requires only a sincere and informed desire to rise above the fray by the most direct path—the high road. The group sentiments include patience, tolerance, refusal to judge, and willingness to listen. Above all, such a group must commit to totally respecting confidentiality.

The Purposes of the Practice Circle

In the preceding chapters you have written your Personal Manifesto and examined your emotions and thought patterns. The Practice Circle rounds out and completes your healing via helpful interchange with like-minded people. It accomplishes this in four primary ways:

By allowing for disclosure.

By allowing you to get and offer different perspectives.

By providing a community of support.

By helping you become part of a stimulating collective conscious-ness.

The Value of Disclosure in the Healing Process

Self-disclosure to like-minded people shows a willingness to heal that usually signals a willingness to change. Disclosure opens the door to allow others to help us heal the wounds of divorce. When we disclose our negative emotions—which include revenge, hate, anger, blame, self-blame, and guilt—in this group we do it because we want another perspective. The Practice Circle provides a format for that part of us that wants to reduce negativity.

When you disclose something to someone in the group, it builds trust. This can stimulate others to disclose things to you, and eventually this mutual trust builds a sense of community.

In this group you become more aware of behavior you are in denial about by seeing it in others. If you give the group permission (see the "hot seat" item in "How to Start a Practice Circle" below), you may get feedback about your behavior or become aware of times when you are deceiving yourself. Something someone says may spark an insight for you. You may hear about behavior you don't want to duplicate or actions you really admire; either way you may be able to gather useful ideas for fortifying your Personal Manifesto.

Mutual fears are flushed out by disclosure. It is helpful and bonding to know that everyone is contaminated by the same fears at their starting point.

The Value of Other People's Behavior and Opinions

Seeing other people's struggles can help us de-emphasize our own self-concern. Danish philosopher and theologian Søren Kierkegaard said, "We can't become who we are because of who we are." In other words, we all create our own blind spots over time and out of necessity. Sometimes when we watch others' struggles that are similar to our own, we may be able to glimpse around the blind spot. We can't see something in ourselves, but we may be able to see it in others. This increases our ability to have insights.

As you learn about other people's behavior, you may begin to reflect about your own behavior. It is as if you have someone else role-playing your behavior before you do it. So when a similar thing happens to you, you will have already reflected about the situation, and this will slow down your reactive responses. As you observe members of the group moving through their healing process, it is as if you are observing living theater. Consider the Practice Circle as a type of theater of learning.

Other people in the Practice Circle offer different ways of looking at a situation. This helps counteract the fear of having no options. We get to observe others creatively going beyond conflict and interpreting life events in different ways. In Alcoholic Anonymous they call this sharing your experience, strength, and hope.

You will develop a sense of curiosity about how others are managing their healing process. This will keep you open to new ideas and information. You will continually be reinforced to "stay open."

The Value of a Community of Support in the Healing Process

As you start to change, you will want to be understood, which will lead to the desire for different connections and networks. You will find yourself moving away from people who increase your stress and negativity and toward those who encourage your better self.

In the group participants can express themselves authentically and without fear of judgment. As the group members share their ideas, concerns, hopes, or even specific problems, they discover the supportive bond of community. This community addresses the need for support that previously was provided by marriage. In addition, the experience pool of the group can be the source of practical advice about esoteric issues involved in divorce, such as visitation and child behavior problems.

Collective Consciousness

Ultimately people want to believe their journey and the suffering they have endured have a purpose. They know they have a story to tell, and in the Practice Circle they can tell others what they have learned. Therefore, to be part of this Practice Circle is to know that you are part of cultural change.

The process of divorce in our culture is often locked into a life-diminishing process. The Practice Circle is a way of reaching out instead of being hooked into that process. Many people shut down as a result of conflict, but participating in a Practice Circle keeps you from shutting down. You will be motivated and supported to focus on the future rather than a difficult past. If you stay open and reach out, you can be ready to absorb your future.

Practice Circles are in essence a grassroots movement to change perceptions about how to deal with the destabilizing effects of crisis, specifically breakup and divorce. They can help immunize us against the combative culture of divorce. If these new perspectives can touch one out of every two of us who participates in marriage (the divorce statistics), a substantial cultural change will be created. New ideas are the movers of history and culture—not just for personal healing, but toward positive changes in social consciousness.

How to Start a Practice Circle

Where are these potential practice partners to be found? With divorce rates so high, you are likely to come into contact with fellow travelers at every turn. The first step to developing your own Practice Circle may be as simple as sharing a cup of coffee with a friend from the carpool, another parent from your child's class or soccer team, or even someone you run into at your attorney's office. If you cannot assemble a group from those you know, you can run an ad in a local newspaper or put a notice on the community bulletin board in your local church, supermarket, or coffee shop. Your local radio station might even run a public-service announcement for you.

Here are some steps for getting the word out:

- Find a location for your first meeting. Space is often available at churches, schools, hospitals, or restaurants. After your first meeting, other people may have ideas for locations.
- Write and post or send out an announcement that says when and where the group will meet. Include your number or e-mail address and ask potential responders to contact you, so you will know the size of the group.
- Keep a list of first names of those who respond and their contact numbers for follow-up.

The meeting itself might be formatted as follows:

- Ideally, a Practice Circle consists of two to six people. It can be larger, but that tends to make it less intimate. Perhaps begin with a silent or guided meditation. Remind everyone at the beginning of each meeting of the importance of building trust by keeping everything said in the meeting completely confidential. Suggest that participants not share anything in the meeting that could be detrimental to their court case. You might tell your attorney you are attending a support group and ask if there is anything you should not reveal.

- Individuals take turns checking in: bringing the group up-to-date on their current dilemmas, progress, or setbacks. Many groups use a formula called PIES for getting current with each other on topics of physical, intellectual, emotional, and spiritual well-being. These check-ins should be about two minutes long. Nobody should interrupt or comment during a check-in.

- Read a portion of a chapter of *The Good Karma Divorce* or listen to a portion of the book's audiotapes for about ten minutes. Ideally the topic will be agreed upon in advance. You may choose do any of the various exercises in each chapter, or just follow the sequence of the chapters in the book. Possible topics include: writing your Personal Manifesto, how to ask a difficult spouse to write a Civility Contract with you, how to get your point across without criticizing, and talking to your children about the divorce.

- The participants then take turns commenting on the topic. These comments can include their experience with the topic in the past or currently, what has worked, what hasn't, or anything else they want to say that is relevant. The group should agree on a time limit for comments. It is not advisable to encourage people to talk about the nuances of their legal case.

- Any participant in the group may request a "hot seat" by asking the others to offer advice on particular situation or future action. Otherwise no one should be judgmental about someone else's thoughts or actions.

- Near the end of the first meeting, decide how often you want to meet, what time, and what day.
- Close with a discussion of the next meeting's topic and a short meditation.

Internet Compassion

In a less-complicated world, I would hope that every divorcing individual might find such a group to affiliate with during progress through this difficult territory. I am also pragmatic enough to realize that an in-person, real-time Practice Circle may not be possible or realistic for everyone. There are also those that feel more comfortable with total anonymity. In recognition of this, I have also launched "The Good Karma Divorce Practice Circle," a virtual Practice Circle accessible at www.thegoodkarmadivorcepracticecircle.com.* This site makes use of something I've described as "Internet compassion." It allows a divorcing individual to connect, anonymously, with others in a similar situation to practice the techniques found in *The Good Karma Divorce.*

Whether you choose the virtual Practice Circle or prefer a group that meets in person, the process is the same. Utilizing guided exercises, group-discussion topics, and other practice methodologies, *The Good Karma Divorce* Practice Circle connects every participant to a growing support system based upon positive, effective techniques for preserving respect and civility and safeguarding children from the potential danger inherent in dissolving marriages.

---

* Any communication with this Web site is completely anonymous and confidential. To avoid any conflict, I have no access to it whatsoever.

Acknowledgments

First she supported my idea, then she coached my writing, then reinvigorated my energy. When she was convinced "it was ready," she became the 007 of agents. She was the secret weapon. Susan Raihofer is not only my agent but my friend.

My editor, Gideon Weil, who believed in this project in a way I have never experienced. He had a vision, which gave the book the solid form it would need to have life.

I am enormously grateful to Susan Keiser. I was lucky enough to have this brilliant ally who championed my thoughts, challenged some, made some better, and without which this book would not be the same.

A special thanks to the force of nature, Julia Cameron, who when I told her twenty years ago I couldn't write told me "just start writing . . . I may know more about this than you think." She supported me all this time until I was finally ready to listen.

Harry William Lowrance IV, my former husband, who gave me faith that a Good Karma Divorce is possible.

To my presiding judges—my mentor, Judge Carol Bellows, and Judge Moshe Jacobius, Judge Timothy Evans, and all the Domestic Relations

Judges in Cook County, Illinois. Thank you for your wisdom. I can only hope it was contagious.

Thanks to my attorneys for their loving confrontation when my ideas needed more clarity: Robert Sheridan, Warren Lupel, Linda Mensch, and Mary Hutchings Reed

Thanks to my family at work, Dean Sanders and Deputy Robert Rico, who said to me one day "you should write down those things you say in court."

Many thanks to my friends, who gave me encouragement and helped me with their unique expertise and affection—first, Jim Raim. There are many others I want to mention by name: Jim Baird, Carol Isaak Barden, Amy Jo Berk, Susan Berman, Tim Boyd, Margot Chapman, Wendy Clinard, Natalie DeSurrey, Angela Fomohare, Allen Gerrard, Douglas Gerrard, Susan Hadley, Maryann Kuehl, Martin Lescht, Fay Hartog Levin, Karen Levine, Gregg Mann, Colin Matisse, Kevin McAuliffe, Dr. Leonard Miller, Rebecca Alleman Perez, Mandy Pins, Jeff Rude, Keith Rudman, Susan Russell, Melody Sabatasso, Stephanie Sereles, Lonee G. Star, Diane Stone, Margaret Sullivan, Janis Weiss, Laura Weathersby, Charles Williams, and Brenda Rafferty Yadav.

If this book helps people at all, it is only because my publicists, Suzanne Wickham and Laura Ingman, the best in the business, got the word out.

And of course an enormous thank you to the most important ingredient of all, my editors, Lisa Zuniga and Ron Silverman.

Notes

Chapter 1
Your Personal Manifesto:
The Antidote to the Negative Seductions of Breakup

1. Dr. Leonard Miller, "Was Freud a Scientist?" Seminar, American Behavioral Studies Institute, Beverly Hills, CA, May 2005.

2. National Institute on Alcohol Abuse and Alcoholism Clinical Trials; govitentifier NCT00818939, University of Texas Health Center, Houston, TX, March 2009.

3. UCLA Newsroom 7, "Harsh Family Environment May Adversely Affect Brain's Response to Threat, UCLA Psychologists Report," Health sciences news release, Los Angeles, CA.

4. Julia Cameron, *The Artist's Way* (New York: Jeremy P. Tarcher/ Putnam, 1992), pp. 217–224.

Chapter 2
The Process: Reclaiming Your Power

1. Daniel Goleman, "Friends for Life: An Emerging Biology of Emotional Healing," *New York Times*, October 10, 2006.

2. Carol Pearson, "New Studies Highlight the Emotional and Physiological Bond Between Married Couples," study, Washington, D.C.

February 23, 2006, Dr. Richard Davidson University of Wisconsin, VOANews.com.

Chapter 3
Criticism: A Flood in the Mouth, a River with No Banks

1. John M. Gottman, Julie Schwartz Gottman, and Joan DeClaire, *Ten Lessons to Transform Your Marriage* (New York: Three Rivers Press, 2006).

Chapter 4
The Stains of Heartbreak: Hot-, Warm-, or Cold-Blooded Anger

1. Eckhart Tolle, *A New Earth: Awakening to Your Life's Purpose* (New York: Dutton Publishing, 2005), p. 144.
2. Janice Williams, "Anger Increases Risk of Heart Attack," study, May 2000, University of North Carolina, Chapel Hill.
3. Robert Sapolsky, *Why Zebras Don't Get Ulcers* (New York: W. H. Freeman and Company, 1994), pp. 20–36, 58–68, 132–164.
4. John Ratey, *SPARK: The Revolutionary Science of Exercise and the Brain* (New York: Little Brown and Company, 2008), p. 352.

Chapter 5
Carnival Mirrors: Betrayal

1. Annie Dillard, *The Maytrees* (New York: HarperCollins, 2007), p. 92.

Chapter 6
Mood Lighting: Emotions as a Source of Illumination

1. His Holiness the Dalai Lama, "Notes on a Teaching," August 30, 2007.
2. Tolle, *A New Earth*, p. 90.
3. Lynne McTaggart, *The Field* (New York: HarperCollins, 2008).

Chapter 7
Forgiveness: Weapon of Mass Construction

1. Alvaro Pascual-Leone, "The Brain Fitness Program," VHS (PBS Home Video).

Chapter 9
Damage to Children: Developing the Heroic in Your Parenting

1. Judith Wallenstein, Julia Lewis, and Sandra Blakeslee, *The Unexpected Legacy of Divorce* (New York: Hyperion, 2000), pp. 67–68.
2. Thich Nhat Hanh, Mindfulness Retreat, Estes Park, CO, August 21, 2007.
3. Wallenstein et. al., *The Unexpected Legacy of Divorce*, p. 5.

Chapter 10
Your Child's Wounded World

1. Wallenstein et. al., *The Unexpected Legacy of Divorce*, p. xxix.
2. Wallenstein et. al., *The Unexpected Legacy of Divorce*, pp. xxxiv–xxxv.
3. Wallenstein et. al., *The Unexpected Legacy of Divorce*, p. xxxv.
4. Beth Erickson, *Longing for Dad: Father Loss and Its Impact* (Deerfield Beach, FL: Health Communication Inc., 1998), pp. 146–65.

Chapter 15
Karma and the Recycling of Human Relationships

1. Norman Doidge, *The Brain That Changes Itself* (New York: Penguin Books, 2007), pp. 45–92.